QUARRY BANK &
THE DELPH

NED WILLIAMS &
THE MOUNT PLEASANT LOCAL HISTORY GROUP

MARIE BILLINGHAM, MARY BROOKES, CAROL COBB, KATH DAY, KEN DAY, JACK HILL,
DEREK HOMER, MARGARET HOMER, JOHN JAMES, JOCELYN LLOYD, PETER LLOYD,
SHEILA MARSHALL, JOAN PEARSON, NORMA PEARSON, LYNDA LAKER, MIKE PERKINS,
PHOEBE POOLE, MARGARET PRIEST, DOREEN RUTTER, DENNIS RYDES

The History Press

THE BLACK COUNTRY SOCIETY

The Black Country Society is proud to be associated with **The History Press** of Stroud. In 1994 the society was invited to collaborate in what has proved to be a highly successful publishing partnership, namely the extension of the *Britain in Old Photographs* series into the Black Country. In this joint venture the Black Country Society has played an important role in establishing and developing a major contribution to the region's photographic archives by encouraging society members to compile books of photographs on the area or town in which they live.

The first book in the Black Country series was *Wednesbury in Old Photographs* by Ian Bott, launched by Lord Archer of Sandwell in November 1994. Since then over 70 Black Country titles have been published. The total number of photographs contained in these books is in excess of 13,000, suggesting that the whole collection is probably the largest regional photographic survey of its type in any part of the country to date.

The society, which now has over 2,500 members worldwide, organises a yearly programme of activities. There are six venues in the Black Country where evening meetings are held on a monthly basis from September to April. In the summer months, there are fortnightly guided evening walks in the Black Country and its green borderland, and there is also a full programme of excursions further afield by car. Details of all these activities are to be found on the society's website, **www.blackcountrysociety.co.uk**, and in *The Blackcountryman*, the quarterly magazine that is distributed to all members.

PO Box 71 · Kingswinford · West Midlands DY6 9YN

Title page photograph: The Chairman of Brierley Hill UDC, Cllr Sid Husslebee, crowns the 1963 Quarry Bank Carnival Queen, watched by Cllr Horace Hadley (on the left), who was Chairman of the Carnival Committee and a shop-keeper in New Street. Cllr Bill Henley is on the right. Bill Henley was also a Quarry Bank man, and was a foreman at Hanke's Engineering Factory. Both councillors did a lot of work for the Brighter Old Age Committee. The Carnival Queen was Anne Andrews from 71 Acres Road, and her attendants were Sandra Morris, from 40 Charles Road, and Cynthia Raybould from Oak Street. The picture was taken at the Carnival Ball on Monday 26 August 1963 as a week-long series of events began – and culminating in a very wet Bank Holiday Saturday when Pat Phoenix (Elsie Tanner from *Coronation Street*) came along to the Gala. (*County Express*)

First published 2009
Reprinted 2010

The History Press
The Mill, Brimscombe Port
Stroud, Gloucestershire, GL5 2QG
www.thehistorypress.co.uk

© Ned Williams, 2010

The right of Ned Williams to be identified as the Author of this work has been asserted in accordance with the Copyrights, Designs and Patents Act 1988.

British Library Cataloguing in Publication Data.
A catalogue record for this book is available from the British Library.

ISBN 978 0 7524 5134 3

Typesetting and origination by The History Press
Printed in Great Britain

CONTENTS

MARRIED IN QUARRY BANK

In *Quarry Bank Past & Present* the Mount Pleasant Local History Group used a series of local wedding photographs to show how they record changing fashions decade by decade, explain links between local families, and illustrate the variety of venues used for such events. At one time it was a choice between the parish church and the nearest register office. One by one the Nonconformist chapels obtained licenses to hold weddings and in this book we have featured the first weddings to take place at three Quarry Bank chapels: Cradley Forge, Birch Coppice, and the Congregational Chapel in the High Street.

George Smith married Jean Hadley at Cradley Forge Methodist Chapel on 17 May 1958. The bridesmaids are Brenda Hadley, the bride's sister (who reappears on page 14 as Sunday School leader), Norma Hadley and Hilary Capewell, the bride's cousins. The pageboy is Peter Garrat, and also visible is Arnold Hadley, the bride's father, who had applied for the chapel's marriage license, and paid for it. The picture shows the porch in its unextended form, and a row of houses appear in the background which are not there now. *(George & Jean Smith)*

INTRODUCTION

Welcome to this new book produced by the Mount Pleasant Local History Group. This introduction will tell you a little about the book and its subject, and the story of the group of people who have produced it.

This is our fifth book about Quarry Bank, so we are looking into some matters that we have considered before, but also asking you to accompany us into a new exploration of The Delph. We are all well aware of the fact that The Delph is really part of Brierley Hill, and was certainly never part of Quarry Bank in terms of local government. However, it is an area that has largely been ignored by local historians and we feel there are several ways in which it has strong links with Quarry Bank. In the past there was two-way traffic between The Delph and Quarry Bank as some children in the former chose to come to Mount Pleasant for their education, and some adults from the latter made their way down into The Delph to work in its

A book like this is often obsessed with boundaries. Here we see the Mousesweet Brook dividing Quarry Bank from Cradley Heath as it passes beneath Forge Lane. It travels under a bridge that seems to have moved and been changed a number of times, while trying to deal with problems of flooding, and the changing road use in the area. *(Ned Williams)*

pits and brickyards. From 1934 onwards, both areas have been part of the much enlarged Brierley Hill, and subsequently became part of Dudley MBC.

So, how do we put together a book that encompasses Quarry Bank and The Delph? The answer is quite simple. This book takes you on a journey from Quarry Bank's eastern frontier at Cradley Forge, up the town's High Street to the zig-zag crossroads by The Blue Ball. From there we make our way along Mount Pleasant – the crest of Quarry Bank's 'bonk' – and then down into The Delph.

The Cradley Forge was located at the confluence of the Mousesweet Brook and the River Stour, both of which help define the boundaries of Quarry Bank. Dud Dudley was alleged to have built the forge by the beginning of the seventeenth century, and it survived until the end of 1906. Damming the Mousesweet Brook just below its confluence with the Black Brook created the Cradley Pool. The pool provided a head of water to drive the forge hammers, and also determined the way in which small squatters' settlements developed on either bank – at Mushroom Green and Birch Coppice. These small settlements of nailers, later colliers and chain-makers, were the kind of scattered hamlets that had to be welded into a single township of Quarry Bank during the nineteenth century. The dam across the pool also created a route, now replicated by Forge Lane, linking Quarry Bank with Cradley Heath, although in the past it was equally important to maintain links with Cradley on the other side of the Stour.

As we leave Cradley Forge behind and ascend the High Street, you will see that we have created two areas for the purpose of this book: Lower and Upper Quarry Bank. Lower Quarry Bank consists of the High Street up to the junction with Sheffield Street on one side, and to Queen Street on the other, plus the territories on either side of the

The tree in the centre of this 1950s picture of the High Street marks the boundary between 'upper' and 'lower' Quarry Bank. *(MPLHG)*

Roller Cycle Racing takes over the tennis courts in Stevens Park at the Quarry Bank Carnival of 1957. We focus on the development of the park in a later chapter, and in trying to understand how the park came to Quarry Bank we find ourselves looking into the interwoven lives of the Quarry Bankers themselves. The investigations undertaken by members of the Mount Pleasant Local History Group have always proceeded on the 'one thing leads to another' principle. Recently the group has followed Dennis Ryde's enquiries into the history of the Quarry Bank Diamonds – a team of cycle speedway enthusiasts established in 1960. Together with enthusiasts from Cradley Heath, they created a cycle track at Hickman's Plateau, sometimes known as 'The Table Top', in an area of wasteland near Doulton's Clay Pit at The Saltwells. *(MPLHG)*

High Street. This means that Lower Quarry Bank stretches out to Birch Coppice on one side, and out to Bob's Coppice and Dunn's Bank on the other.

Upper Quarry Bank consists of the 'top' of the High Street and the corresponding territories on either side – in one direction stretching out to the 'top' of Coppice Lane, and the other taking in Stevens Park. A look at Stevens Park has led us to create a separate chapter on the park and some of the town's history to which it is interrelated. This includes the families of Quarry Bank who have featured both in the story of the park and the town, and the events in the park that have reflected and celebrated Quarry Bank's sense of community.

In creating two sub-sections of Quarry Bank, you might wonder whether they are different. Lower Quarry Bank consists of some of the older, more scattered communities that were eventually gathered together to create the town. Cradley Forge not only takes us back to the early stages of the Industrial Revolution, as outlined above, it also takes us back to the earliest stirrings of Nonconformity. First the independents came to this spot, and then the Methodists, mainly Primitive, as at New Street, or New Connexion as at the Forge itself. It follows that Lower Quarry Bank became home to the Liberal Club, and its twentieth-century protégé, the Labour Club.

On the other hand, Upper Quarry Bank became home to the new parish church – built by the Church of England in the mid-1840s in response to the population growth of the district, and the developing sense of the town's identity. The 'top' of the High Street hosts the commercial hub of Quarry Bank, and the Conservative Club. All this developed a few hundred yards from the zig-zag crossroads that might have become the centre of Quarry Bank. For all the urbanisation of Quarry Bank, it is interesting to note that only one bank, the Midland, opened a mere 'sub-branch' in the High Street.

Mount Pleasant runs astride the 'top of the bonk', once with farmland stretching down to the banks of the Stour, and with an area on the other side that was heavily mined for coal. The latter – the 'basin' of the Tipsyford Brook – was turned into derelict waste by the mining, until eventually cleaned up to provide a location for the Merry Hill shopping complex. Right out at the end of Mount Pleasant the Wesleyan Methodists built a chapel as early as 1828, probably sited deliberately as an 'out-of-town' location that brought in a congregation from a wide area. A little ribbon development along Mount Pleasant took place in the nineteenth century but the areas alongside it, and along the Amblecote Road, only became truly urbanised in the twentieth century.

Crossing the Quarry Bank boundary, we descend from Mount Pleasant into The Delph. 'Descend' is the right word, both physically and historically! The Delph was 'another world'; a basin created by the Colbourne Brook running westwards towards Amblecote. But any sense of a natural landscape belonging to this area has to be forgotten; The Delph became a man-made landscape, created by the exploitation of two minerals: coal and clay. The Dudley No. 1 Canal came to the foot of the Delph Locks in June 1771, and then waited to be met by the Stourbridge Canal, which came into use six months later. In the 1850s the landscape was altered once again as the railway was pushed from Stourbridge Junction up to Dudley. As the line climbed towards Brettell Lane, it traversed an embankment that cut off the eastern side of The Delph from the same kind of territory that headed westwards into Amblecote. In the nineteenth century the landscape was greatly 'turned over' once again as open-cast mining ripped up the landscape on either side of the railway line. By then the pits had closed and the brickworks were in rapid decline – and once the landscape 'settled', new housing development has transformed the area.

The canal bridge at Black Delph – at the foot of the canal locks – is at the centre of this area. At one time the road from Mount Pleasant to the bridge was called Delph Road, and from the bridge to Silver End it became Lower Delph Road. The world on one side of Lower Delph Road is strongly linked to Brierley Hill by steep roads, and our survey takes us no further than the top of these roads. Nor do we quite make it to Silver End! The other side of Lower Delph Road includes the gasworks site and this has been of more interest to us.

The really fascinating part of The Delph was served by minor lanes: Turk Street, Delph Lane and Turner's Lane, that all converge with Delph Road on the approach to the canal bridge. These lanes led into the scattered settlements on the Amblecote Road side of the valley. This housing had to compete with the pits and the 'pitbonks', and the brickyards and their claypits. It was a tough, unstable, physical environment and the Church of England bravely decided to build a mission in the middle of it all in 1886.

In recent years, much of The Delph has been lost and buried beneath the vast new Withymoor Village. Our interest was stimulated by the fact that this was maybe the last chance to speak to people who knew The Delph as it was. These people did not take many photographs, or write copious memoirs, but their memories may provide a last glimpse of The Delph as a distinctive area.

This journey across Quarry Bank and down into The Delph means that we have had to miss out many other parts of Quarry Bank, but many of these have been covered in our previous books. Some parts of Quarry Bank, such as Caledonia, or Dunns Bank, or Mears Coppice, are as unchronicled as The Delph, but we have already given them our attention.

Our history group began to meet every Friday afternoon at Mount Pleasant School in the autumn of 1997, at the invitation of the school's head teacher, Gail Bedford. Our first aim was to produce a history of the school for the building's 110th anniversary. This was achieved with the production of *110 Not Out!* in 1998. By then our interests had broadened to include every part of Quarry Bank, and we had begun meeting under the auspices of the Workers' Educational Association (WEA), thanks to the efforts of WEA organiser Ken Godfrey. In this way we continued our work and produced three more books: *Quarry Bank in Old Photographs* (1998), *What's Happened to Quarry Bank?* (1999) and *Quarry Bank: Past and Present* (2003).

Over the ten years we have been meeting, we have joined various activities designed to preserve or promote a sense of community in Quarry Bank. At one time such

In 2001 the MPLHG became involved in an 'Enjoying Life in Quarry Bank' project and welcomed these three visitors to our stand in the Community Centre: Roy Smith, Debra Shipley MP and Councillor Brian Cotterill. Debra points to her 'I love Quarry Bank' badge – produced by the History Group, and worn in Parliament! *(Ned Williams)*

At the launch of *What's Happened to Quarry Bank?* on 3 November 1999, Stan Hill of the Black Country Society, wearing the chain of office of the Chair of Brierley Hill UDC, re-creates a 1961 photograph of Councillor Homer at the Quarry Bank Gala, in the company of Eileen Hadlington (Carnival Queen) Pat Cox and Maureen Hill (attendants) – wearing the original tiaras! *(John James)*

work seemed to be making good progress, but in recent years it has faced a number of setbacks. Currently Quarry Bank has suffered a series of blows as institutions like the post office and the public library have closed. Local discussions about regeneration and about caring for the facilities like Stevens Park have to be reconciled with a feeling that the future of Quarry Bank still has many uncertainties. At the same time, the History Group faced a crisis when the WEA withdrew the kind of support we had previously enjoyed. Events almost destroyed the group, but somehow it has continued to meet and still enjoy the hospitality of Mount Pleasant School. Over the years, some members of the group have died, some have left to take up other interests or moved away, and yet new faces still appear at our door to share new information, or to lead us into new lines of enquiry. Some come as visitors, some come to stay!

The History Group has always wanted to share an interest in the present and future of Quarry Bank as well as look at its past. We have tried to record and take note of recent change in the area, and this in turn has given us a 'past and present' approach to history – in other words, in the absence of anything better, we will look at a recent picture to try and understand changes that have taken place.

The work of a History Group is never finished, but right now we are adding our last full stop to this particular book, hoping that you will enjoy it, and will come and explore Quarry Bank and The Delph.

1

LOWER QUARRY BANK

We begin our journey across Quarry Bank and out into The Delph by approaching the town from Cradley Heath, having made our way along Forge Lane. The frontier is crossed at the point where the Mousesweet Brook passes under Forge Lane, but nowadays you have to work quite hard to be aware of this. Just before the First World War, the junction of Forge Lane and Quarry Bank High Street went through the first of several modifications, and today the alignment brings High Street down into the valley and only gently swings slightly into Forge Lane. Originally the High Street swung much more to the right into what we would now call Cradley Forge. This would have led the traveller into Maypole Hill and eventually to the Netherend area of Cradley. At one time, therefore, the Waggon & Horses was at the lowest point of the High Street, and almost opposite was the small, square Methodist Chapel of Cradley Forge. The latter has completely vanished – replaced by the building 'on top of the bank' and reached via Hammer Bank.

Hidden in the trees behind the Waggon & Horses is the confluence of the Stour (left to right) and the Mousesweet Brook (running from the foreground). The photographer is standing in Cradley Heath (Sandwell) looking across to Quarry Bank. The far bank is in Cradley. *(Ned Williams)*

The original alignment of the lowest part of Quarry Bank High Street once occupied the space now filled with grass, as it turned towards Cradley and passed the Waggon & Horses. Behind the Waggon & Horses is the wooded area, illustrated on the previous page, where the Mousesweet Brook runs into the Stour. This was probably the site of Dud Dudley's water-powered sitting mill where thin sheets of iron were slit into rods for sale to the nail-makers. The present-day building is possibly the third on the site and the road, as well as being realigned, has probably been widened. *(Ned Williams)*

Lower High Street, Quarry Bank, 2009. The bus is passing houses that belong to (and are numbered in sequence with) the pre-war council houses in Woodland Avenue. The iron sign and steps on the extreme right welcome explorers to the area known as 'The Pipes' and the original dam that held back the waters of the Mousesweet Brook to form the Cradley Pool, described in more detail in our previous books. *(Ned Williams)*

Young Vernon Pewton takes up a trowel in 1928 and joins in the foundation stonelaying ceremony at Cradley Forge Methodist Chapel's new Sunday School in Hammer Bank. Ten years later, when the original chapel closed to facilitate road-widening, the Sunday School building began to 'double' as chapel – which it has continued to do right up to the present. Vernon was later killed during the Second World War. *(Joyce Parkes)*

Nonconformists had been represented at Cradley Forge since the days when an independent chapel was built here known as the Pensnett Meeting House. Later, the New Connexion Methodists took over at Cradley Forge, but of course this former Sunday School building dates only from 1928. Note the later extensions on either side of the porch. *(Ned Williams)*

The Cradley Forge 'Sunday School Reunion' service of 27 April 2008 united present-day scholars with old scholars and effectively filled the chapel. *(Ned Williams)*

Brenda Guest addresses the four present-day Sunday School scholars at Cradley Forge on 27 April 2008 at the Reunion Service. Georgia, Megan, Alex and Leoni are also seen here singing to the congregation. *(Ned Williams)*

Roger Pirie was born in Dudley and his early interest in photography was enhanced by work at Dudley Odeon and then K.G. Corfield's 35mm camera factory in Wolverhampton. After National Service he joined Midland Red as a photographer in their Film Unit. After nine years' work for Midland Red, Roger opened his own studios in Dudley, which operated between 1968 and 1973. In 1973 he married Jean Faulkner and they moved to 129 Lower High Street, Quarry Bank.

The shop had previously been Mr Bragger's greengrocer's shop but Roger fitted it out as a photographer's studio. The Piries lived on the premises until 1983 and became well-known local wedding and commercial photographers – based at this shop until the summer of 2006. On the right we see Roger outside the premises and, below, in the dark room. *(John James)*

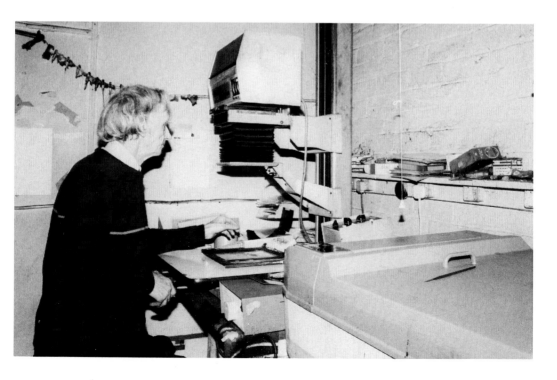

The lower end of Quarry Bank's High Street is fairly straight as it descends from the old school (seen in the distance). This view, taken in about 1930, precedes the building of the Coronet cinema, which was to occupy the space on the right from 1933 until 1960. When the picture was taken a small chainshop stood beyond the tree. *(Joyce Webb)*

Another picture that begs to be included despite the fact that is not a very sharp image! A Midland Red single-decker passes the Elephant & Castle in the 1950s as it descends the lower part of the High Street, having passed the junction with New Street on the left. In the foreground to the right is the front of the Coronet cinema – the blinds drawn down to shade the two shops built into its frontage. In the distance is the old infants school building, at the point where the High Street bends slightly to the left. This building, now demolished, was Quarry Bank's first school and had opened in 1872, only two years after the local school board had been established. Just beyond the cinema is the entrance to Rose Hill. QB Bikes now stands on this corner. *(MPLHG Collection)*

The front and back of the Coronet's programme brochure for October 1954. The local advertising is as interesting as the films being shown: two businesses in Stour Hill, Wallins' shoe shop, Hadley's coaches, Shaw's soft drinks, etc. *(B. Clark)*

The Elephant & Castle, on the corner of Rose Hill. In the 1950s the landlord was Harold Leslie Cartwright. The pub probably came into being in the mid-nineteenth century as the High Street was developing into the form we know. *(MPLHG)*

Rose Hill photographed in September 2003, before these old cottages (nos 13–16) were demolished to make way for new houses. Rose Hill made its way from the High Street up to the site of Saltwells No. 33 Colliery, probably worked from about 1890 to 1912. Rose Hill becomes a narrow track beyond this point, and leads to Dunn's smallholding. The row of cottages carried the date 1835. *(Ned Williams)*

Quarry Bank Primary School as seen from the High Street in April 2004, when demolition of the original 1872 building was underway. The bell tower – already shorn from the building – was supposed to have been preserved, but without success. *(John James)*

Quarry Bank School's netball team, 1924. The girl on the left of the front row was Florence Felton (1910–35) who was later a well-known Sunday School teacher at Cradley Forge. The teachers are Miss Locke and Miss Woodridge, and other pupils include Fanny Parry, Emily Hall, Hilda Maybury and Edith Bloomer. *(Joan Thornburgh's Collection)*

Quarry Bank School cricket team, 1931. Seen here are Messrs Cresswell, Glaze, Bennett, Whylie, Dandle, Attwood, Southern, Johnson, Priest, Attwood, Edwards, Brookes (with ball, captain) and Goodwin. Staff in the back row include Mr Wood, Mr Tate, Billy Scriven and Mr Badger, the headmaster (with arms folded). *(W. Brookes' Collection)*

This group photograph taken in the playground at Quarry Bank Junior School in the 1950s is interesting as the angle chosen looks out towards Cradley and Homer Hill on the horizon. *(MPLHG)*

Just above the Liberal Club we come to the recently extended premises of Quarry Bank's carpet dealer: Walter Wall, seen in the top photograph in February 1998. Terry Bellis was a carpet fitter who had a sideline in delivering turf. It was the latter which introduced him to Quarry Bank! One Friday in March 1966 he set up his carpet business at 157 High Street, rented from Mrs North who had previously run it as The Valeting Service. The first day's sole business was a £10 donation to the local Scouts' tombola, but the following Monday three 'Scout Mums' became his first customers. Since then Terry has purchased the adjoining shops, nos 154, 155 and 156 and recently no. 157 (formerly separated from no. 156 by a gap). In the lower photograph, Terry's younger son, Jeremy (on the left), now owns the business, joined by elder son Christopher, and grandsons Mitchell and Danny. They are seen here with Marcia and Terry in this 2009 picture by the extended premises. *(John James)*

James Hadley outside his shop at
159–60 High Street. James came to
live at no. 159 when he was three,
the premises then being used as
booking office and travel agency for
the family's coaching firm. Having
trained as an upholsterer, James
set up his business, Wear & Tear, in
Cradley Heath, and came to Quarry
Bank in 1992 when the shop at
no. 160, formerly The Tackle Box,
became available. By then Hadley's
booking office next door had closed
(in 1990) so James has used both
shops. No. 160 had once been
Walter Gilder's grocery shop.
(John James)

Coppice Lane descends into the valley of the Black Brook in the same way that High Street descends the 'bank' towards the Stour and its tributaries. Therefore the Coppice Lane Schools seem to be part of Upper Quarry Bank, while the Birch Coppice Chapel seems to be part of Lower Quarry Bank. The chapel was 'planted' by the Primitive Methodists in New Street in 1884, reinforcing the view that it belongs to Lower Quarry Bank. From 1888 until 1957 the congregation met in a 'tin tabernacle' but this was replaced in 1958 with the present brick building. *(Chapel Archives)*

The Sunday School anniversary, seen here on 5 May 2008, was part of the building's 50th birthday celebrations. *(Ned Williams)*

The first wedding at Birch Coppice Chapel took place on 5 April 1947 when Mary Flohr married Claude Roussell in the tin chapel – the day after the license for conducting weddings arrived. Ironically the bride and groom then went round to the Methodist Chapel in Dudley Wood to take this photograph! The material to make all the clothes was 'on coupons' and was supplied by Chattin & Hawtin of Brierley Hill. *(From the collection of Mary Roussell)*

The Revd David Alford joins the Sunday School children in preparing to cut the birthday cake on 17 August 2008. The date was the celebration of the 50th anniversary of the brick chapel used by the Birch Coppice Methodists. *(Ned Williams)*

At one time New Street was the busy commercial heart of Lower Quarry Bank, although it looks somewhat sleepy in this 1947 picture. The shop on the right is Hadley's shop – on the corner of Queen Street, seen in better detail in the picture below where three German friends (left) pose with Gladys and Norman Hadley, and Gladys's friend, Gwen Harris. *(Norma Pearson)*

Stretching from Cradley Forge up to New Street are the streets that once formed 'Lower Quarry Bank' (Evers Street, Brick Kiln Street, Stour Hill, Hill Street, New Street, Queen Street, etc.). Similarly – on the other side of the High Street – Woodland Avenue and Rose Hill form part of Lower Quarry Bank. At one time, rather separated from the rest of Quarry Bank, was the small community of Birch Coppice. An extension to Sheffield Street and Woodland Avenue eventually brought Birch Coppice 'into the fold'.

At one time a large tree grew out of the pavement in the High Street, just above Sheffield Street and this can be regarded as the frontier between the two halves of Quarry Bank.

GLADYS HADLEY

Gladys Hadley née Trueman was born in Waterfall Lane, Blackheath, in 1912. She left school at fourteen and went to work in the Swallow Raincoat factory in Birmingham. She first came to Quarry Bank to teach piano to Joyce and Joan Hadley. Piano-playing made little progress, but Gladys met their brother Norman, whom she married. They first lived in a little cottage at 38 New Street, but six years later, in 1939, they moved into a brand new home, which they had built at 35 New Street.

Burt and Ettie Hadley, Gladys's in-laws, left New Street to keep the Hare & Hounds at Kidderminster, so Gladys took over their shop at 122 New Street, on the corner of Queen Street. Gladys ran the lock-up shop, raised five children, helped run the family coach business (also based in New Street), was secretary to the Ladies' Class at Cradley Forge Chapel, and was also chapel organist from 1970 until 1996. She had also been pianist for the Cradley Forge Operatic Society.

Gladys's shop was used as a community centre. If the chair was occupied, customers would sit on sacks of potatoes or milk crates, and put the world to rights. Gladys looked after customers, especially during the time of food rationing, and made sure everyone had a treat for Christmas. She would deliver groceries and then work all night on the sewing machine to make sure her daughters had new dresses for the Sunday School anniversary – plus white ribbons for their hair.

Perhaps Gladys did not want to live on into the twenty-first century – she died on Millennium Eve, and her family, numbering about forty, decided to celebrate her life with a fireworks and champagne send-off.

Gladys Hadley at home on the piano in the 1990s. *(Norma Pearson)*

Hadley's Coaches in New Street were one of four Quarry Bank-based coach companies. Sometimes their fleet spilled out onto local streets. *Above*: An AEC Regent III of the early 1950s is parked in Queen Street, just round the corner from Hadley's shop. The vehicle was probably on loan to Hadley's from Watt's (Prospect) Coach Company of The Lye. In the background we see a tantalising glimpse of Queen Street. *Below*: From a window above Hadley's shop we see coaches lined up in New Street, and once again we see a glimpse of the street, including the large factory that once existed there. *(Photos courtesy of Geoff Hingley and Norma Pearson)*

The Primitive Methodist Chapel of 1902/3. It was designed by Abraham Ramsell, replacing an earlier building of 1860 which had subsided in about 1897, and dominated the Quarry Bank end of New Street. Ramsell's other works included the Dudley Opera House. Behind it was a substantial Sunday School building. Subsidence struck again and the chapel closed at the end of the 1970s. No trace of it remains. *(MPLHG)*

The Victorian houses beyond the site of the chapel have survived but have been much rebuilt, although this August 2003 picture looking down past Brick Kiln Street towards the White Horse gives little impression of how much New Street has changed. *(Ned Williams)*

The White Horse was damaged by fire in 2005, and it looked as if New Street would lose its fine Victorian pub, but here it is seen in June 2005, two weeks prior to the reopening. *(Ned Williams)*

When this picture was taken in March 2004, the butcher's shop on the left had already closed, as well as the one-time fish and chip shop next door; both were returning to residential use. Between New Street and the Stour are the old streets of Lower Quarry Bank: Ever Street, Brick Kiln Street, and Stour Hill, which together with Maughan Street and Queen Street formed this distinct sub-section of Quarry Bank. *(Ned Williams)*

Left: The little lamp-oil shop on the corner of New Street and Maughan Street was rather eclipsed by the large premises of Joe Goodwin's grocery store nearby, and was probably closed by the time this picture was taken in the early 1950s. It was eventually demolished and the shed-like premises of Quarry Bank Glass Ltd occupied the site for some time.

Below: Customers posed outside the Red Lion at 35 Maughan Street in the 1900s, when the licensee was Samuel Homer. Today the building is a private house – still calling itself the Red Lion. *(MPLHG)*

2

UPPER QUARRY BANK

Coming up the hill one enters Upper Quarry Bank by passing the site of the boundary tree on the right, just above Sheffield Street, and passing the New Inn on the left. Upper Quarry Bank is home to the parish church, the Conservative Club and the Congregationalists – contrasted with the three Methodist chapels, the Labour Club, and the Liberal Club, which were at home in the lower half of the town.

At this end of the High Street one is more aware of the Victorian development of the town and the streets to the north of the High Street are laid out in strict Victorian rectilinear style: Victoria Road, Church Street, and the top of Queen Street, Maughan Street, and lower part of King Street.

In the twentieth century, Upper Quarry Bank has also been home to the post office and the public library – both closed while this book was being compiled – and has been the retail hub of the town. It is here that you gain the strongest impression of how Quarry Bank grew and prospered, and correspondingly, of how the town has struggled to cope with forces unleashed towards the end of the twentieth century. The shops, the church, the library and the nearby park all feature in any consideration of Quarry Bank as a living urban community.

This locally produced 1950s postcard of the High Street provides a glimpse of the tree that marked the boundary between Lower and Upper Quarry Bank. It stood outside Groves's Butcher's shop, now Jewess's shop. Beyond the tree is the junction with Sheffield Street. *(John James's Collection)*

The New Inn, on the corner of Queen Street, marks the start of Upper Quarry Bank on that side of the road. Between the wars it was run by Henry Stevens, who brewed his own beer on the premises, and also ran the Queens Head. More recently, David Cooper has energetically run it. *(Ned Williams)*

The shops on the south side of this steeply graded section of the High Street face Sheffield Street and the Community Centre. Cloud Nine Balloons occupy premises that were previously Freddie Field's Central Hairdressing. Both pictures were taken in 1998. *(Ned Williams)*

Cloud Nine Balloons moved out of the premises glimpsed on the previous page and moved into this larger shop – which had once been an optician's and then a branch of the Midland Bank. The business was the brainchild of Kath Harvey, seen on the right, who had first seen balloons used to decorative effect at a London wedding. Kath, and her daughter Maxine Cooper (left), studied the art and eventually launched the business from a garage in Wychbury Road. It was an instant success and they first moved into the premises seen on the opposite page. *(John James)*

Maxine Cooper and Kath Harvey at Cloud Nine Balloons in 2008. Although their first love is balloons, their shop now sells cards, gifts and wrapping paper, and organises all aspects of weddings, parties and family events, from invitations to cakes. *(John James)*

Above: Quarry Bank's busy upper High Street in the 1970s, from the Dental Laboratory (the ex-Vine pub), on the corner of Victoria Road, on the right, to Homer's electrical store on the left. *(John James)*

Left: Opposite the junction with Victoria Road is the Congregational Church. Here we see a 125th anniversary banner being put up over the entrance on 23 February 2009. One hundred and twenty-five years takes us back to 1884 when an independent congregation began to meet in an ex-soap factory on the Mount Pleasant side of Merry Hill. They moved to a purpose-built chapel in Z Street in 1897. Z Street subsequently became Chapel Street and the congregation built this church in 1935 – leaving the Z Street building, behind it at lower level, to become the Sunday School. Philip Williams and Alan Southall are seen on the ladder while Angela Hodgetts looks on. *(John James)*

Quarry Bank Congregationalists held their 125th anniversary service on 1 March 2009, and assembled outside the church for a group photograph. The congregation, who have remained outside the United Reformed Church in which Congregationalists and Presbyterians amalgamated, have always proudly maintained a Sunday School. In 1967 the Sunday School was able to move from the 1897 building into new premises built alongside the church, facing the High Street. *(John James)*

The first wedding at Quarry Bank Congregational Church was celebrated on 29 January 1966, when Alan Southall and Jill Hall were married. Left to right: Gillian Bishop and Nellie Southall, Vivienne Priest, David Penn (best man), the bride and groom, Laura Hall, Samuel Bradley, Joan Bradley and Lorraine Downton.
(Alan Southall)

Pictures of the Dudley Co-operative Society's premises in Quarry Bank High Street have been hard to find – perhaps as a result of being on the shadowy side of the street. This picture was taken in early morning sunlight on 27 June 1949, when Kendrick Transport Ltd of Dudley was providing coaches for a Co-operative Society outing (see page 40). As well as providing a glimpse of the Co-op's shopfront, we can admire Kendrick's Leyland half-cab coach, JFD 191, which was then about a year old. *(Bernice Giles)*

For many years the Quarry Bank Post Office was on the southern side of the High Street at no. 195. Mr H. Light was the post-master and he also ran the annual flower show. Before this the post office had been at 48 High Street, and had been run by a Mr Griffiths, and at one time it had been in Thorns Road. It can be difficult to keep track of Quarry Bank's past post offices and their locations. This picture was taken in the summer of 1994 just before the post office moved to the other side of the road. *(John James)*

Mr and Mrs Bennett are seen here at the newspaper counter in the 1970s. They operated a news agency at 41–2 High Street, Quarry Bank, until it was taken over by Adrian and Melanie Guy in 1994 on becoming the new home of the post office. Like all such shops it sold a wide range of goods, including confectionery and stationery. *(John James)*

Left: Adrian and Melanie Guy, proprietors of Guy's Newsagents, 41 High Street, July 1994. *(Express & Star)*

Below: By March 2000, 41 High Street had become a Spar shop, the frontage had been remodelled and, when this picture was taken, the letters on the front of the building saying 'Quarry Bank Post Office' had just been removed. A new standard Post Office sign has appeared on the left of the shop front and lottery tickets are now included in the variety of goods on sale. *(John James)*

Quarry Bank Post Office photographed on the day it closed, 3 February 2009. The post office had been run by Mrs Naranjan Kaur and Naginder Singh since 2004, and the shop has been run by Mrs Balwinder Kaur and Mr Vishavjit Singh. Local people opposed the closure of their post office, but, as in many other places, their opposition could not save it. However, the shop continues to operate the convenience store side of its business under the Premier franchise. *(John James)*

Sally Wasdell's pharmacy in the 1970s, now Murray's Chemists. To the left is the Church Tavern on the corner of Church Road. This pub has now returned to its original name, having been known as the Nailmaker for several years! *(John James)*

Once again the Co-op Society's outing of 27 June 1949 provides more than just a picture of Kendrick Tranpsort's magnificent Dudley-based fleet of coaches – we also have a tantalising glimpse of details of Quarry Bank's High Street. In this case we can just see the original front door and frontage of Quarry Bank's public library on the right, a building originally shared with the police station. *(Bernice Giles)*

Quarry Bank Library photographed in July 1998. The library was opened on 5 February 1939 by Councillor H. Edwards, Chairman of the Library Committee on Brierley Hill UDC, supported by the Quarry Bank councillors who had campaigned for it: Simeon Wood, Alf Workman and Ralph Homer. At some stage the front of the building was modernised, possibly when it ceased to also be a police station. *(Ned Williams)*

Right: Quarry Bank Library launched weekly coffee mornings for a while before it finally closed. The 'regulars', seen here on Thursday morning 8 January 2009, were generally opposed to the library's closure – which took effect two days later on 10 January 2009. The library had always been important to Quarry Bank and its provision had been fiercely fought for during the first few years after Quarry Bank was absorbed by Brierley Hill. *(Express & Star)*

Below: Despite protests, Quarry Bank Library closed on Saturday 10 January 2009. Here we see Assistant Librarian, Sue Lee, locking the front door for the last time. Minimal library services were then provided at the Community Centre. *(John James)*

Just behind Quarry Bank Library was Dudley Council's Estate Office. Like the library and post office, this also had to close at the beginning of 2009. Cllr Brian Cotterill lined up with the Estate Office staff on the day the office closed, 3 January 2009. Left to right: Sue Hill, Bonnie Ginifer, Cllr Cotterill, Sue Roberts and Beryl Bowater. *(John James)*

Christ Church, Quarry Bank, seen from Park Road. This striking church built in cream refractory bricks was consecrated on 2 March 1847, illustrating that Quarry Bank had sufficiently grown by that time to need a parish church of its own. *(Ned Williams)*

A postcard view of the interior of Christ Church. Designed by Thomas Smith in the Early English style popular with the Church Commissioners, it has gone through several modifications over the years. The window was a bequest from Jesse Billingham, installed when the chancel was extended in 1900 after a fire. Ernest Stevens later provided a brass lectern, and the Revd Mr McNulty (1893–1920), seen top left, provided the stone pulpit. *(MPLHG)*

The famous Quarry Bank Choirboys' Strike of 1967. In the September of that year eighteen members of the choir, aged between nine and fourteen, refused to sing when two probationers were excluded from the choir. The vicar, the Revd Mr Larkin, and the choirmaster, Michael Thompson, met the strikers behind closed doors and the matter was agreeably resolved! *(MPLHG)*

Nick Knowles working in the High Street greengrocer's shop owned by his parents, John and Norma Knowles, photographed in the 1970s. When an employee got married, Nick and his parents could not leave the shop unattended, hence the need to take a wedding picture outside the premises! The building is now used by Mario's pizza takeaway. *(Both pictures John James)*

Harry Scrivens set up his butchery in Quarry Bank High Street, two doors away from Marsh & Baxter's shop, on 9 January 1967. Harry eventually moved into the ex-Marsh & Baxter shop – seen here in the picture above – and in 1989 began demolishing the three shops next door – between Mary's Fashions and the Royal Oak. He had converted the latter into two shops earlier in the 1980s. *(John James)*

As work proceeded on this row of shops in 1989, damage to the adjoining building and subsidence caused problems. Harry Scrivens had to take on the entire row of buildings and face higher bills than he had anticipated! Compare this picture with photos on pages 13 and 24 in *Quarry Bank in Old Photographs*, and see *Quarry Bank Past & Present* for more details on Mary's Fashions and Firkins' bread and cake shop. The picture also shows the junction with Oak Street, now opened out by a new island. *(H. Scrivens Collection)*

Mary's Fashion was featured in *Quarry Bank Past & Present* when the shop was run by Pat Stevens. Pat ran the shop for thirty-eight years having taken over from her mother, Mary Gash, who had first opened the shop. Here we see the present proprietor, Donna Evans-Hadley, at the shop doorway on 29 May 2007. Donna is Quarry Bank born and bred and worked next door at Firkins' Bakery shop for ten years. In 2006 Firkins was taken over by the Wollaston Bakery and Donna left to take over Mary's Fashions. *(John James)*

Below: Barry Whitehouse in T.P. Services on 2 March 2009. The shop sells hardware, flowers, pet food, sweets, etc. Having run the shop since 1990, Barry feels he has witnessed the decline of the High Street. *(John James)*

From Mary's Fashions up to Take a Bite on the corner of Oak Street, the original shops subsided in the 1970s and this new block was built in their place. As well as T.P. Services there is an amazing fancy dress shop. Here, on the corner of Oak Street, is a sandwich shop run by Mr Scrivens' wife and daughter on the site of what was once the Royal Oak. *(John James)*

Mr and Mrs Scrivens, and their daughter Alison, in their Take a Bite shop at the top of Quarry Bank High Street on 3 March 2009. *(John James)*

Just beyond the parish church, the High Street used to suddenly veer to the left, and Oak Street went off to the right. The corner of Park Road, originally known as Bower Lane, can be seen on the left in this late 1940s picture. On the right is the last of three villa residences known as Salisbury House. This area has been considerably opened out now that High Street forges straight ahead at this point. *(MPLHG)*

Salisbury House, which had been built in 1892, is seen here being demolished in January 1998 in order to straighten the High Street and to make way for a mini traffic island. Behind the terrace is the blind factory, which now marks the corner of Oak Street. Among the graves in the foreground to the right is one with a circular cross. This is the grave of Paul Lacey, a nineteenth-century music hall artiste, who had the stage name Charles Godfrey. *(Ned Williams)*

As a result of the recent straightening of Quarry Bank's High Street, the entrance to Oak Street has been opened out revealing the premises of The Blindmakers and, on the far side of the road, premises which had once been the home of Taylor's crisp factory. David Taylor started making his crisps here in 1949, having previously made them at the back of his fish and chip shop in Old Hill. Staff prepared and fried the crisps in machinery devised by David Taylor, and eventually four delivery vans were required to deal with demand for their crisps, packets of cheese and biscuits, scratchings and nuts and raisins. *(John James)*

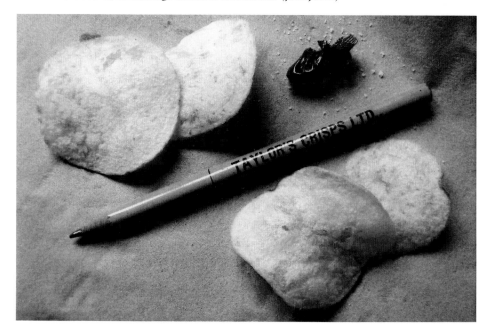

In the area around Oak Street, Sun Street and Merry Hill, there is a small industrial quarter of Upper Quarry Bank. Noah Bloomer's chainshop in Oak Street carried on making chain in the traditional way until the mid-1970s. Here in January 1974 we see Dick Bloomer forging a link with his nephew Robert Bloomer. *(Express & Star)*

Noah Bloomer & Son set up their chainmaking factory in Oak Street in 1887 and it grew to include thirty hearths, a machine shop, warehousing and testing facilities. They developed a speciality in short-link chain using the name Samson Brand, and this was exported all over the world.

Below: Galvaniser John Withers dips a metal bird feeder into a zinc bath at the Bird Stevens & Co. works in 2009. The works extends from Sun Street to Merry Hill. *(Express & Star)*

The High Street turned past the building seen on page 48, past a tenement building known as 'the High Buildings' (demolished in 1967), and then Hawkeswood's ironmongers shop, now Jantino's. (See *Quarry Bank in Old Photographs*, pages 11 and 12). After those buildings came the Sun, seen here in May 1998. This elegant 1930s pub has now been demolished and even the Travel West Midlands bus is now history. *(Ned Williams)*

The Blue Ball Inn stood at the original junction of the High Street with the old turnpike road from Dudley to Worcester, which it faced. The staggered crossroads here formed the geographical centre of Quarry Bank, where the north–south route of the turnpike was crossed by the more locally important west–east road from the top of the bank down into the Stour Valley. The pub is marked on early maps, but little is known of its history. Here it is being demolished in 1960 to make way for its modern replacement, which had been built behind it. *(MPLHG)*

The new Blue Ball subsequently closed and was metamorphosed into an Indian restaurant – seen here preparing to reopen as such on 26 August 2003. At one stage the old Blue Ball sign was taken down, then it was 'rescued', but then disappeared again! *(Ned Williams)*

This June 1952 picture helps us to visualise the crossroads as it once was. Bearing in mind the halt sign on the road in the foreground marks the entrance to Thorns Avenue, it can be seen how narrow Thorns Road was before the widening, and then the rebuilding of this junction in 1998. The wooden building on the right was once used by the British Legion, later by the Scouts, and then the plot was laid out as a Garden of Memory. Compare this view with the picture on page 9 of *Quarry Bank in Old Photographs.*)*(MPLHG)*

The Blue Ball crossroads in January 1998, before the top of High Street was closed off and the crossroads realigned, and opened out to cope with traffic to and from the Merry Hill Shopping Centre. *(Ned Williams)*

The widening of Merry Hill, in progress in May 1998, completely altered the topography of this area on both sides of the road, and resulted in demolition of property in Merry Hill and Mount Pleasant. Merry Hill was the name of this stretch of the old turnpike road long before the shopping complex adopted the name, and it ran down to the Robin Hood, via the junction with Coppice Lane which can be seen in the distance. *(Ned Williams)*

An aerial view of Coppice Lane shows the Coppice Lane Island and the old turnpike road (Merry Hill) running down past the Robin Hood in the top half of the picture, *c.* 1974. Coming down Coppice Lane, on the left, we also see the location of the boys' and girls' secondary schools on either side of the road. Bottom left are the houses of the White City, an early Quarry Bank council estate, and to the right are the newer houses of the Birch Avenue Estate. Two Woods Lane follows the old boundary of Quarry Bank UDC, top left, and the 'empty' fields, top right, have been transformed by the building of the Merry Hill Shopping Centre. *(W.Boyd)*

Looking down Victoria Road from Coppice Lane, with the 'new' cemetery (of 1903 vintage) behind the trees on the right. (Compare this 2008 view with the picture on page 34 of *Quarry Bank Past & Present*). *(Ned Williams)*

Coppice Lane runs roughly parallel to the High Street and therefore also runs through an upper and lower section of Quarry Bank. In 1900 it was relatively undeveloped, although Victoria Road had pushed through from the High Street and the parish church had acquired a new cemetery alongside it. Six imposing houses were built at the Victoria Road junction at the turn of the twenty-first century, seen here in 2009. *(Ned Williams)*

The boys' and girls' secondary schools, on either side of Coppice Lane, were built in 1932 and were formally opened the following year. They were amalgamated in 1969 and became a comprehensive in 1975, by which time the move to Stockwell Road was underway and Thorns Community College was being created. Here we see the staff at the boys' school in about 1960. In the middle is Mr Jeavons, the headmaster. *(Vera Dunn Collection)*

Girls from the Coppice Lane Secondary School are seen here in about 1953 on a visit to Dudley Castle. Both of these pictures belong to the era of gymslips and school berets! *(MPLHG)*

Pupils at Coppice Secondary School in 1953. Back row, left to right: Betty Lewis, Barbara Priest, Margaret Harris, Vera Bloomer, Irene Dunn, Judith Weaver, Elsie Willets, Gladys Cooper. Front row: Joyce Rooker, Janet Cooper, Ann Bradley, Margaret Jenkins, Jean Cartwright. *(Margaret Homer)*

3

STEVENS PARK:
GATEWAY TO HISTORY

Quarry Bank acquired a public park as a result of the generosity of Ernest Stevens, proprietor of the Judge Enamelware works in Cradley Heath. A wealthy local businessman and resident of Prescot House in Stourbridge, Stevens' connection with Quarry Bank was the result of two things. Firstly he had grown up in Quarry Bank where his father had a business in Brick Kiln Street, and secondly he had married Mary who was a member of the Wesleyan Methodist congregation at Mount Pleasant. For the first ten years of their married life they lived at the Sycamores in Thorns Road.

After the First World War, Ernest Stevens decided to give some land off Thorns Road to Quarry Bank Urban District Council on the understanding that they would create a

The grand gateway to Stevens Park in Thorns Road is now little used, the entrance from Park Road having become more important. Hill & Smith Ltd of Harts Hill made these gates, and those at Mary Stevens Park in Stourbridge. They also supplied the ironwork for the bandstand. *(MPLHG)*

public works scheme to landscape the area and transform it into a public park. The land itself was worked-out colliery waste – generally regarded as too unstable to be built on.

Landscaping the area and creating a park and recreation ground was put under the direction of a Mr F.A. Furber, the Urban District Council's surveyor. Work was not completed in time for the official opening, possibly because Ernest Stevens had donated more land in the interim and the project was therefore larger than first anticipated. The official opening was scheduled for 16 July 1921 and was to be a key event in the history of Quarry Bank. It was therefore organised on quite a grand scale and looking back on it all these years later provides us with an opportunity of re-creating a picture of life in Quarry Bank at that time.

Quarry Bank had been conducting its own affairs since the formation of the Urban District Council in 1894, and the nineteenth century had witnessed the development of a number of social institutions around churches, schools, political clubs, etc., so that the community was quite complex by this time, even though the First World War had turned many things topsy-turvy.

Coronations and Sunday School anniversaries had established traditions of great public parades, and organisations like Scouts, the Boys' Brigade and adult Friendly Societies all turned out to support such events. This is difficult to imagine at a time when even local carnivals have declined and disappeared in many areas, including Quarry Bank. Thus it was that the opening ceremony planned for Stevens Park began with a parade.

A 2.00 p.m. on 17 July 1921, a procession was assembled in the schoolyard of the old infants' school in Lower High Street. The procession was going to be almost a mile in length and therefore took considerable organising. It was marshalled by Joseph Westwood who found himself organising the annual Friendly Society parades, or 'carnivals', that were organised in Quarry Bank every year between the wars in aid of funds for local hospitals, particularly the Corbett Hospital. The procession was led by the Quarry Bank Silver Band, a marching band that had begun life in the late 1880s as part of a contemporary temperance movement. For fifty years its president was Walter Wootton, the local photographer.

Behind the band came elected members and officials of the UDC. Albert Shaw was Chairman of the Council and J.E. Dunn was Chairman of the Parks Committee. They were closely followed by A. Homfray, Council Clerk, who was a solicitor based in Cradley Heath, and J.G. Billingham, the Deputy Chairman of the Council, closely shadowed by H. Thorneycroft who was Deputy Council Clerk and Secretary to the Parks Committee, and C. Williams who was Treasurer to the Council. Mr Furber and Mr J.A. Long, who was Ernest Stevens's architect, also marched in front of the rest of the council. The councillors were H. Dunn, Stan Yardley, Simeon Wood, James Foxall, J.C. Mason, G. Court, J.T. Whiley, T. Griffiths, Ralph Homer, W.H. Ingley, Edwin Smith, and A.W. Green. It might seem unnecessary to name them all but many were well-known Quarry Bank figures who made quite a contribution to the life of the community, and many have descendants who still live locally today. There were also named representatives of Brierley Hill and Rowley Regis present.

Behind this throng came members of the Rowley Regis St John Ambulance Brigade led by Sergeant Shaw and then about fifty Quarry Bank ex-servicemen led by Captain Flavell. The procession made its way up the High Street and was already turning into Thorns Road before the rear of the procession had left the infants' school. Once again the quality of local newspaper reporting enables us to go into greater detail about the parade giving the modern reader a glimpse of just how many organisations existed in Quarry Bank. Joseph Westwood's role as marshal guaranteed that the branches of local Friendly Societies were well represented – none of which exist today.

The Quarry Bank lodge of the Free Gardeners was known as the Lily in the Bower Lodge and they were followed by members of the Rose in June Lodge of the Druids and several local lodges of Buffaloes. The Quarry Bank Boys' Brigade, led by Lt. Jones, was present but at the time no Scout troop existed in the town so troops from neighbouring towns came along in great number. The rest of the procession was made up of school children from Quarry Bank (High Street) and Mount Pleasant. They were accompanied by their teachers which meant that well-known head teachers were also present: Miss F. Woolridge of the girls' school, Mr I. Badger of the boys' school, Miss Wood of the infants' school and Mr W.E. Hunt of Mount Pleasant School. All these names will be known to Quarry Bankers over a certain age!

The procession might seem to have included every single person in Quarry Bank but apparently not as there were considerable crowds watching its progress. These were kept in order by Police Superintendents Robotham and Haynes. Possibly many parents turned out to watch their children march by, each waving a Union Jack and dressed in their Sunday best. By the time the procession and everybody else had crowded into the park, the number present was estimated to be nearly 7,000 people.

Cheers broke out as Mr and Mrs Stevens mounted the platform, escorted by Messrs Shaw and Dunn. The official party must have taken some time to find a place on the temporary platform, and they were joined by the vicar, the Revd Mr Vizard, and the Revd J.W. Scott of the Primitive Methodists. The band broke out with the national anthem and Councillor Shaw began the proceedings. He welcomed Mr and Mrs Stevens and urged everyone present to love and respect their new park, which was basically a desire to see it protected from vandalism – a plea that can be understood by the Friends of the Park today. He was sure, 'that the park would add to the health, strength and virility of the populace of Good Old Quarry Bank.'

Mrs Mary Stevens responded and declared the park open, and was then presented with a bouquet of pink carnations by Miss Dorothy Thorneycroft.

Joyce Parkes, Councillors Brian Cotterill and Davis Sparks – representing the Friends of Stevens Park – study plans while posing in front of the 1925 bandstand.
(*Express & Star*)

Messrs Dunn and Court then made speeches echoing sentiments expressed by Councillor Shaw but presented a motion of gratitude to Mr and Mrs Stevens. While everyone was cheering, Ernest Stevens rose to his feet. Once he had expressed his pleasure in being present and reciprocated everyone's good will, Ernest Stevens went on to explain some of his motivation in seeking to create the park. He recalled his boyhood in Quarry Bank and explained how he and his friends had been forced to play cricket by the roadside with home-made bat and ball. He hoped the post-war generation would benefit from better prosperity and from the facilities the park set out to provide.

After the speeches, the official party retreated to the refreshment tent and the public at large explored the new park, listened to the Quarry Bank Silver Band, or made purchases from the fruit stalls set up by the refreshment tent. The bandstand was a later addition to the park so only a temporary platform was provided in 1921.

THE STEVENS PARK SHELTER

Mary Stevens' death prompted her husband Ernest to continue in his role as public benefactor, but as we have seen in the case of the bandstand, these gestures were now in memory of her. She seems to have had a similar influence on the womenfolk of Quarry Bank, and they also decided to undertake a project that would perpetuate her memory. The project took the form of providing a shelter and pavilion in Quarry Bank's park.

It is usually the menfolk who dominated public affairs at that time, and the shelter project was definitely undertaken to counter that fact. The organising and the collecting of funds was all carried out by the womenfolk of Quarry Bank and, as the official opening approached, it was obvious that this was their chance to make sure their names were given their proper place in the town's history. As luck would have it, Cllr Stan Yardley was unable to be there and Mrs Yardley was able to lead the proceedings, and Mrs Deeley was asked to perform the opening itself. Ernest Stevens and the husbands of Quarry Bank were going to be there, but the women were determined not to be overshadowed.

The shelter had been designed by G.H. Plant, based on the work of Mr Long – Ernest Stevens' own architect, and was built by J.M. Tate, the well-known local builder.

The opening took place on Saturday 17 October 1931 and despite cold weather the park was well-filled for the event. The proceedings began with singing the hymn, 'Praise the Lord, it is good to praise' and Mrs Ogg then read prayers and some scripture. The Quarry Bank Silver Band, conducted by Mr P. Cooper, provided the music. Mrs Yardley then read an apology for absence from her husband and paid tributes to several pioneers of the project who had not lived to see it come to completion: Mrs Turner, Mrs Hickman and Mrs Pardoe. She hoped the shelter would always remind people of 'a noble woman who lived and worked among them for so many years.'

Mrs Deeley then made her speech, declared the building open, and handed it over to the Chairman of the UDC to receive it on behalf of the people of Quarry Bank. The UDC chairman was Councillor Herbert Dunn, and at last the men were been allowed to speak. Inevitably Ernest Stevens then spoke and very graciously complimented the women on the success of the project. He hoped it would be the first of several shelters and others would follow the example and lead of the women of Quarry Bank. In conclusion, Ernest Stevens said, 'I thank you all with a full heart for the great tribute you have paid to the noble woman whose life's work you sum up so admirably by inscribing on this gift: And she went about doing good.' Councillor Dunn and Mr Plant formerly proposed a motion of thanks to the womenfolk and then everyone adjourned to the tea tent.

So, who were the women of Quarry Bank who had done so much fund-raising and kept the project alive for five years? Thanks to the *County Express* we can provide plenty of names: Mrs McCarthy, the vicar's wife, Mrs Ogg, the Primitive Methodist Minister's wife, Mrs Dunn, Mrs Bird, Mrs Claydon, Mrs Thompson, Mrs Johnson, Mrs Crow, Mrs Maybury, Mrs Totney, Mrs Belfield, Mrs Hickman, Mrs Stringer, Mrs Griffiths, Mrs Allport, Mrs Smith (Thorns Road), Mrs Pearson, Mrs Genner, Mrs Guest, Mrs Aston, Mrs Jones, Mrs Beaman, Mrs Cox, Mrs Price, Mrs Bloor, Mrs Goodwin (Maughan Street), Mrs Robin (Kinver), Mrs Billingham, Mrs Cartwright, Mrs Westwood, Mrs Radford, Mrs Wood, Mrs Shaw, Mrs Rowley and her friends from Lye, Mrs Grove and Mrs Bate.

THE PEACE MEMORIAL

The most outstanding feature of Stevens Park was the Peace Memorial. This was unveiled on Saturday 24 October 1931, only a week after the opening of the shelter. About 2,000 people filled the park to see the memorial unveiled by the Dean of Worcester, Dr W. Moore, and once again Ernest Stevens played a major part in the event and the finances.

On this occasion the proceedings started in the parish church where a memorial service was held, conducted by the vicar, the Revd Mr McCarthy, assisted by ministers from the three major branches of Methodism: the Revd Mr Phillips from the Wesleyans, the Revd Mr Ogg from the 'Prims' and the Revd Mr Bone from the United. The congregation included fifty members of the local branch of the British Legion. When the service finished, everyone lined up to march to the park under the supervision of Police Sergeant Hodgkiss.

The Quarry Bank Peace Memorial, seen on the previous page and again here, is still regularly used on Remembrance Sunday. There is a parade down to the park from the parish church and a ceremony held at the memorial. Here we see the standards of the Cubs, Scouts and British Legion lowered during the ceremony of November 2004. *(Ned Williams)*

The house in the background of the top picture is seen here in a 1920s postcard sold in Quarry Bank. For a time, Quarry Bank Urban District Council met in this building in Park Road. Quarry Bank was absorbed into Brierley Hill in 1934. *(Ken Rock Collection)*

The vicar and curate from Christ Church, plus audience, watch a Dove of Peace being released from the bandstand on 10 July 2005 during a band concert held to commemorate sixty years since the ending of the Second World War. The bandstand was opened on 22 August 1925 by Ernest Stevens in memory of his wife. *(Ned Williams)*

They were met at the memorial by the official party led by Ernest Stevens, the Dean, and Councillor Herbert Dunn, Chairman of the UDC, plus many other representatives of the UDC, the County Council, and neighbouring authorities. Another service was conducted at the memorial including hymns sung by the hundred-strong choir, conducted by Joseph Bloomer and accompanied by Mr C.A. Hawkeswood on a portable organ. The Dean of Worcester then dedicated and unveiled the memorial and the 'Last Post' was sounded. Ex-servicemen then dropped poppies by the side of a wreath laid by Owen Stevens, and then the relatives of the fallen placed their wreaths on the memorial. Once again the ceremony was followed by tea in the tent.

The memorial was conceived by Alfred Long, the local architect from West Bromwich, but who had not lived to see the shelter and memorial opened. The brick and concrete foundations were constructed by Messrs Cooper & Son of Blackheath. The stonework was carved and erected by C.R. Davies and Sons of Old Hill. The bronze figure of Christ was sculpted by George Wade of London, whose daughters attended the ceremony. At the time there was no other memorial quite like it, particularly because it stressed the importance of peace as well as the sacrifice of those who had died in war. It is not clear how much Ernest Stevens had contributed to the cost of the memorial, but once again there is little doubt that his generosity had made the memorial a real possibility.

WHO RAN QUARRY BANK?

From the establishment of local boards in the mid-nineteenth century, to the creation of the Urban District Council in 1894, and to its demise in 1934, Quarry Bank was led by hard-working members of a number of key local families, often connected by marriage, serving each other in business, and sometimes united by religious affiliation.

Take William Sidaway who became Chairman of the UDC in 1901. He was born in Quarry Bank in 1843. He was a draper and clothier in the High Street and his wife, Caroline, came from another prominent local family, the Hazlehursts. Then there's

Jesse Billingham, one-time resident of the house now used as the vicarage – he was born in Quarry Bank in 1827 and became an important local brewer and maltster. After his wife's death in 1897 he paid for the east window of Quarry Bank church in her memory (see page 43 of *Quarry Bank in Old Photographs*). He served on the council for twenty years and then on Staffordshire County Council. He was QBUDC Deputy Chairman when the park was opened in 1921.

HERBERT DUNN

As well as the Yardleys and the Shaws and the Deeleys, Councillor Herbert Dunn was also at the opening of Stevens Park in 1921. To follow the life of Herbert Dunn is to wander into the maze of local family and business, political, sporting, social and religious connections that make up the life of a small town. We first encounter Herbert Dunn on page 46 of *Quarry Bank in Old Photographs* where he is seen as Men's Movement Leader and lay-reader at Christ Church, following in the footsteps of his father Ben Dunn who had been Sunday School Superintendent (see page 50 of *Quarry Bank in Old Photographs*). On page 88 of that book we featured him as a Managing Director of Jury Holloware.

Herbert Dunn (*c.* 1886–1963). A life-long member of the congregation at Christ Church, he followed in the footsteps of his father. He was a keen sportsman, playing cricket and later golf. He was elected to Quarry Bank Urban District Council and rose to become its leader. At Jury Holloware in Thorns Road, he rose to become a Managing Director. He married Frances in 1901 and his son John, known as Jack, was equally devoted to the company, became a director in about 1949 and 'died in harness' in 1966.

Quarry Bank cricketers in about 1924, with Herbert Dunn seated in the centre of the front row, with the lad seated in front of him. Jack Dunn is seated on the left hand side, end of the front row.

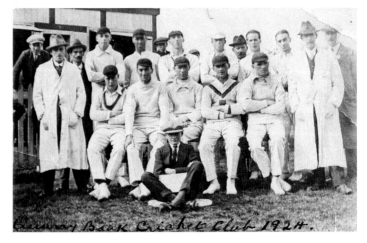

Family connections. On 30 March 1932 Herbert Dunn's son, Jack, married Hilda Allport. Left to right: Herbert Dunn, Harry Hawkeswood, Jack and Hilda, Ernest Allport. The ladies are Frances Dunn, Gladys Allport, Mabel Dunn and Beatrice Allport. This picture was taken at 126 Thorns Road, the same location as the picture on the cover of *Quarry Bank Past & Present*.

Herbert and Francis Dunn celebrate their Golden Wedding at 126 Thorns Road in 1951. Jack and Hilda are now on the left of the picture. The couple dedicated a window at Christ Church on the same day. Jack worked at 'the Jury' until his death in 1966, at the age of sixty-three. *(All pictures in this section from the collection of Jocelyn Lloyd)*

More connections. Ernest Allport, seen top right of the previous page, is seen here with his wife Beatrice and daughter Gladys at 161 Lower High Street, where they ran a hardware store. During the the Second World War Beatrice led the local St John Ambulance Corps. Ernest was brother to two other well-known Allports – Cornelius Allport, who ran a second-hand furniture business in the High Street, and Tom Allport who ran a fish and chip shop at the top of Thorns Road. Ernest and Beatrice's daughter Hilda, married Jack Dunn.

Can you keep up? Jack and Hilda Dunn had one child, Jocelyn, who is seen here marrying Peter Lloyd on 30 March 1957 at Christ Church. Jocelyn had grown up at 120 Thorns Road and had attended Mount Pleasant School and the Red Hill School in Stourbridge. Jocelyn's generation broke the tradition of working for the 'Jury' and of marrying into other well-known Quarry Bank families! Jack Dunn is to the right of the bridesmaid, and Herbert Dunn can be seen just above his granddaughter.

QUARRY BANK AND ITS PARK

Having seen how the development of the park is inter-related with the history of Quarry Bank families and their businesses, we come back to the park itself as a key recreational facility enjoyed by all Quarry Bankers. The key event in all this has been the annual carnival. Between the wars, the carnivals raised money for the local hospital fund. Since the Second World War they have raised funds for other charities, firstly supporting the local Brighter Old Age Committee from 1952 to 1973, and then revived in 1988 for Cancer Research. The last carnival was held in 2000.

Traditional elements of the carnival have included fancy dress competitions and carnival queens, as illustrated by these two pictures of the 1958 Carnival, held on 6 September. Winners in the fancy dress competition: Wendy Street (3rd), Carol Scott (1st), Wendy Genner and Margaret Sutton (joint 2nd). *(MPLHG)*

The Carnival Queen, Margaret Whyatt, and her attendants, Norma Hodgetts and Joan Cooper. About 10,000 people attended the 1958 event and a record sum was raised for the Brighter Old Age Association. *(MPLHG – County Express)*

On 28 June 2008 a Family Fun Day was held in Stevens Park in an attempt to make good community use of the park and re-create the pleasures of the galas and carnivals of the past. An arena was used for martial arts displays, as seen here, as well as jousting by medieval knights! At the back of the field is a line of stalls presented by local community groups, including the History Group. *(Ned Williams)*

Tom Wilson's Fun Fair used to appear in the park at carnival time and still does so even when there is no carnival, and sometimes at a November bonfire. Here the equipment is built up at the Lower Thorns Road entrance to the park on 28 June 2008 for the Family Fun Day. *(Ned Williams)*

4

MOUNT PLEASANT

Mount Pleasant is a street name encountered at various locations in the Black Country. In this case the name was undoubtedly appropriate as the road stretches along the top of the bank, from the High Street's junction with the old turnpike road to a modern island at the entrance to The Delph.

It is now difficult to imagine that this area once seemed separate from the rest of Quarry Bank, and it is also difficult to imagine how wild and undeveloped it might have been when the Wesleyan Methodists came to build their chapel at the western end of this thoroughfare as early as 1828. The Sunday School building at the back of the chapel provided premises for the first Board School in the area (in 1882) – replaced by the present Mount Pleasant School in 1888. The New Connexion Methodists built a chapel almost opposite the school, and later still a small Pentecostal chapel was built nearby. This side of the road was also home to Mount Pleasant's only pub, the Brickmakers Arms.

It was this side of the road which seemed to develop first – leaving the school fairly isolated on the other side during the close of the nineteenth century. However, coal was mined in the Talbot Lane area and made that side of the road very unstable. It therefore became industrialised and remains so today. The school side of the road saw more residential development in the twentieth century.

Marion Prosser, who supplied this picture of Mount Pleasant school children in 1937, could name most pupils. You will find them on page 128.

The demolition of 19 and 21 Mount Pleasant, December 1997. Nos 27, 29 and 31 were also being demolished in the background. No. 23, which cannot be seen from this angle, is now the first house in Mount Pleasant following the road-widening of 1998. The monkey puzzle tree in the background has also disappeared. *(Ned Williams)*

Nos 18 to 28 Mount Pleasant, on the other side of the road, have survived but since this photograph was taken in January 1998 the properties at 30 and 32 (see next page) were demolished (in 2002) and have been replaced with new houses. Beyond, the Brickmakers Arms still exists, but its once-proud bowling green has vanished. *(Ned Williams)*

Mal's Motorcycles at 30–2 Mount Pleasant in July 1998. Mal Hawthorn traded here from 1984 until October 2001, in what was once Ada Dawes's general store. Beyond is the Brickmakers Arms, often known simply as 'The Brick', where Joe Hollis once brewed his own beer at the back of the premises. *(Ned Williams Collection)*

The only known photograph of Mount Pleasant Methodist (New Connexion) Chapel, taken in 1925 just after it had reopened on 12 August. By then it was known as the United Methodist Chapel. The congregation was formed in the mid-1830s from a dissident group of Wesleyans from across the road. From 1907 until 1925 they met in the Sunday School building while the subsidence-affected chapel was rebuilt. The chapel seems to have faded away in the late 1940s, was used as a warehouse for a time, and was derelict for a few years before demolition. *(Ned Williams Collection)*

Houses adjoining the present-day junction with Talbot Lane. No. 56, on the left, follows the general building line but note that the two houses next door are set back and actually occupy the site of the old New Connexion Chapel – the front gardens being the former chapel front yard. Pillars at each side of this frontage are the only evidence of the existence of the chapel. *(Ned Williams)*

The 1888 Mount Pleasant School building, seen here still displaying the monogram of the Kingswinford School Board which had provided it. The bell tower stood above the original infants' entrance, and the location of the school's original hall is suggested by the gable in the foreground, since replaced by the 1992 hall. *(Ned Williams)*

George Whitehouse, Dudley Town Centre Developments Manager, awards Craig Hingley first prize in a competition organised to find a costume for Dudley's 'Keeper of the Fountain'. *(Express & Star)*

Cllr Margaret Wilson, the Mayor of Dudley, joins Eve Harris from Netherton CofE Junior School, and Luke Beardsmore from Mount Pleasant Primary School for a cup of tea in the Mayor's Parlour after receiving 'Pride of Place' environmental certificates. *(Express & Star)*

Mount Pleasant Primary School: the headmistress, Mrs Gail Bedford, takes retirement after completing her final assembly on 19 May 2006. Gail, seen here with the school choir in the school hall, took up the headship in January 1985, three years before the centenary of the present school building. The School Board had actually provided education in Mount Pleasant since 1882 by using the Sunday School building. *(Ned Williams)*

Headmistress, Mrs Gail Bedford, addresses her final farewell assembly on 19 May 2006, in the 1992 school hall. It had been built on the site of an older building of 1912 vintage, which had once been used for woodwork and cookery classes and had later been occupied by Dr Kelly, the school dentist. Mrs Bedford began a four-year modernisation of the school in 1989. *(Ned Williams)*

Jean James (school crossing patrol), Mrs Gail Bedford (retiring head) and Mrs Jo Hartill (incoming head), seen here on 19 May 2006. *(Ned Williams)*

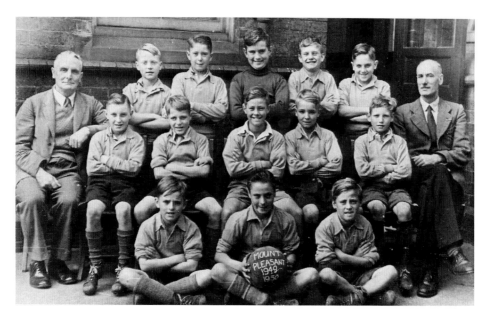

In 1998 the Mount Pleasant Local History Group produced its first book – *The History of Mount Pleasant School* – to coincide with the 110th anniversary of the school's building. The names of head teachers, class teachers and the pupils themselves all poured out as the group researched the history of the school. The first headmaster, Mr Hunt, was a legend and was in post from 1888 until 1930, probably a record that will never be broken. On the left of this picture we see Mr Allchurch, the school's third headmaster, who was the incumbent from 1936 to 1951. On the right is a famous teacher at the school, Mr D'Arcy Jones, who came to the school at the end of the 1920s and left in 1954 to become head at Moor Street, Brierley Hill. In the middle is the 1949/50 football team. *(Pat Mattocks Collection)*

On the left: Mr Geoff Anslow, who became deputy head at Mount Pleasant in 1954 when Mr D'Arcy Jones departed. Here we see him as a class teacher of Class 3 in 1951. *(Pat Mattocks Collection)*

The view along Mount Pleasant from the school to the Wesleyan Methodist Chapel, proudly bearing the date 1828. Compare this 2008 view with the picture on page 29 in *Quarry Bank in Old Photographs*. The front extension to the chapel was added in 1925 as a gift from Ernest Stevens in memory of his wife, Mary, who had been an active member of the chapel's congregation. *(Ned Williams)*

Olive Allchurch, resident of Mount Pleasant and organist at the Wesleyan Chapel, playing at the Sunday School Reunion of 12 May 2002. *(Ned Williams)*

Marjorie Skitt, the late Emma Hanglin and Marlene Watson at the same reunion. *(Ned Williams)*

Ann Brown was once an Anglican worshipping at St James's Church, Eve Hill, Dudley. However, after attending the Jeffreys Crusade at Dudley Town Hall in 1930 she converted to a more Pentecostal style of worship and looked for a site on which to build her own church. She seems to have acted independently of the Assemblies of God and the Bethel Temples, which were both products of the Jeffreys Crusade. Her husband was a chauffeur to the Earl of Dudley and it seems that he was able to persuade the earl to provide a plot of land at the end of Talbot Lane, Mount Pleasant, on which to build Sister Brown's Bethany Temple, which opened in the summer of 1934. *(All pictures Joe Chattin Collection)*

No picture of the Bethany Temple has been found but this post-war Sunday School picture provides a glimpse of the side of the wooden building. Sister Brown died on 15 September 1964 and the temple struggled on under the leadership of Joe Chattin, but falling membership, an ageing building, and occasional vandalism and floods defeated the fellowship by the mid-1970s. A developer re-landscaped the plot and its location is now obscured by industry.

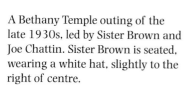

A Bethany Temple outing of the late 1930s, led by Sister Brown and Joe Chattin. Sister Brown is seated, wearing a white hat, slightly to the right of centre.

YOU'VE TRIED THE REST—NOW TRY THE BEST

Biscuit Flavoured Bread, with a Natural Crust.
Delivered in the Blue and Grey Vans. Written
out thus :

HOME BAKERY

George Dunn & Son

QUARRY BANK

Right for Your Neighbour—Right for You, too

Telephone : BRIERLEY HILL 7397

—EAT—

JACK DUNN'S "BREAD"

Scientifically made at

**THE MODEL BAKERY,
MOUNT PLEASANT, QUARRY BANK.**

Inspection invited—Come and see your staff of life made in my
up to date Bakery.

Telephone—Brierley Hill 7498

Perhaps the presence of a corn mill at the end of Mount Pleasant encouraged the growth of local bakeries, or perhaps it was just coincidence. Both George Dunn and Jack Dunn made bread in Mount Pleasant as is proved by these post-war adverts, one from the parish magazine, and one from a Brierley Hill town guide. Just around the corner, George Roberts also produced bread at his Delph Bakery. They were all absorbed by Darby's Bakery of Brettell Lane, trading as Mother's Pride, becoming part of the Rank Hovis McDougall group.

Harold Breese started Brierley Hill Crystal in 1913, and the business is now owned by his grandson, Darryll Hemmings. These premises at the Delph end of Mount Pleasant were used as a showroom, then closed for a while before reopening as the Factory Shop, as seen here in 2004, but are currently used by a tile business. *(John James)*

5

THE DELPH

A t the western end of Mount Pleasant one comes to a busy island, at one time the frontier of Quarry Bank. The Urban District's actual boundary ran to the left down the centre of Mill Street as far as Woods Lane, and to the right along the centre of Amblecote Road. We are taking neither of these routes: we are forging straight ahead into Delph Road. Descending into The Delph we find ourselves in a world that technically was part of Brierley Hill, but it feels neither to be part of

The Delph is most strongly associated with small fireclay mines and brickyards. Brickyard workers were often related and put in long service to their trade. This 1920s group from E.J. & J. Pearson's works are posed in front of one of the many kilns in the area. *(MPLHG)*

that urban district, nor part of Quarry Bank. It is a forgotten area entirely in its own right; a one-time no-man's land of fireclay pits, collieries, brickworks and scattered settlements. Some of the inhabitants ventured into Brierley Hill, others into Quarry Bank – such as those families who sent their children to Mount Pleasant School. The Church of England bravely established a mission in this wilderness but it never grew to be a parish church, much to the frustration of its congregation who relished its independence.

The old landscape of The Delph has been swept away and a vast area of modern housing now obscures its features, and eventually the last generation will have passed away who can still help us put together a picture of life in this area as it was. It was not an area that was well-recorded in photographs or in written records.

We begin our exploration of The Delph by following Delph Road along the 'pub run' from the Vine, to the Black Horse, the Dock & Iron, the Tenth Lock and the Bell. At Black Delph Bridge we explore the canal and the area once dominated by brickworks. Beyond, the Lower Delph Road takes us to the gasworks and to the byways that ascend the slopes of Brierley Hill: Rock's Hill, Little Potter Street and South Street. We then have to retrace our steps to the canal bridge to explore the real complexity of The Delph in a mysterious area once penetrated by Turk Street, Delph Lane and Turner's Lane.

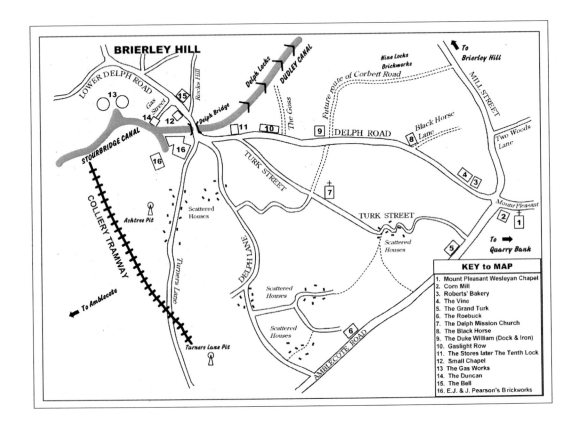

ROBERTS'S BAKERY BY SHEILA MARSHALL

I started work as a general clerk in 1954, at the age of fifteen, at Roberts's Delph Bakery. The bakery was located at the top of Delph Road and was owned by George Roberts. It was a family business and had been passed down to George. Mr Bert Duncombe was the Senior Clerk, Mr Bert Homer was General Manager and Mr Eric Cook was in charge of the delivery side. Mrs May Walker was in charge of making up the confectionery orders.

There were twelve rounds serving all local areas, going out as far as Kinver, Enville, Clent and Blakedown, and the bakery worked two shifts. Between the bakery and the road junction were two council houses. Mr and Mrs Jones occupied the first, and Mrs Jones came in to clean our offices. Next door were Mr and Mrs Chance. Mr Chance used to cook poultry in the bakery's ovens at Christmas. He would take on up to forty turkeys for whoever turned up and cooked them to perfection.

Mr Roberts's aunt lived adjoining the bakery and each day I had to have a cup of tea with her. Aunt Rose, as we called her, was a widow, and on Thursdays I had to take her grocery order to Lawton's general store, a few doors beyond the Vine. I would wait while the order was made up and then take it back to Aunt Rose. She always gave me a packet of Rolos as a thank you. On Mondays I had to walk to The Delph Post Office to purchase National Insurance stamps from Mrs Hopton, and later from Mrs Maybury.

I worked at the Delph Bakery for eight happy years, but in 1962 we were bought out by Rank Hovis McDougall and I moved down to Darby's Bakery in Brettell Lane, along with the staff from J. Dunn & Son and George Dunn & Son – the bakers on Mount Pleasant.

Sheila and a van driver named Pete outside Roberts's Delph Bakery in July 1955. The entrance to the bakery was very modest with no name displayed on the building. It seems that the Roberts family also owned the corn mill on the opposite side of Mount Pleasant, at the junction with Amblecote Road.
(Sheila Marshall)

Tony Whittaker outside the Nine Locks & Chainmaker in 1983 – the pub he built at the island at the junction of Mount Pleasant, Mill Street, Amblecote Road and Delph Road. Tony Whittaker grew up in The Delph. After leaving school he worked for six weeks at Marsh & Baxter's and then at the brickworks – but Tony was born to be a property developer, and later demolished the old Marsh & Baxter's Factory, and later the Delph Gasworks. The latter site became his flagship Delph Road Industrial Estate. The exterior of the Nine Locks & Chainmakers has now been rendered and has been renamed the Corn Exchange, a historical reference to the corn mill that once stood on the site. *(Express & Star)*

The Vine in its rebuilt form in a picture dating from about 1920. The nickname by which the pub is best known, the Bull and Bladder, has its origins in the butcher's shop on the left, at that time leased to W. Cresswell. *(MPLHG)*

By the end of the nineteenth century, the Vine public house, Delph Road, was run down and badly affected by subsidence. In 1905 it was acquired by Daniel and Myra Batham, who were then brewing beer at the King William, in Cole Street, Netherton. Rebuilding commenced in 1911 and one year later it reopened as the Vine Hotel – although still known to everyone as the Bull & Bladder. Brewing on this site has gone from strength to strength and today customers come from far afield for a 'pint of Batham's'. *(Keith Hodgkins)*

Mr Arthur Joseph Batham and his wife, Doris May, at the bar of the Vine. Their grandsons, Tim and Matthew Batham continue to brew Batham's Beer on the premises today. *(MPLHG)*

Traditional home-cooked food has been set out at lunchtime at the Vine for many years. Assistant Manager Eileen Harwood has worked at the Vine for over thirty years. *(Express & Star)*

Melvin Wood has been manager at the Vine since 1990. *(Express & Star)*

Looking up Delph Road, in 2008, towards the Vine from this angle reveals the top of the brewery building, and the small cottages below the pub. Although these cottages have been modernised they are part of the old Delph and once looked out over Gill's Farm on the opposite side of the road. *(Ned Williams)*

Lily and Doris Lawton's shop (sometimes known as Barnsley's) can be seen on the right – now converted back to purely domestic use – and the cottages from here down to the Black Horse show a few signs of Edwardian grandeur and may have been rebuilt at the same time as the Vine. *(Ned Williams)*

The Black Horse in 2008, on the corner of Black Horse Lane, and Delph Road, but not running parallel with the latter, in true Delph style. The earliest known reference to this pub is 1834. *(Ned Williams)*

The Hobson family were associated with the Black Horse for seventy years. Susan Hobson, seen here in the 1950s, came to the Black Horse when she and her husband Arthur left the Grand Turk when Atkinson's license for that pub was transferred to the new Cottage Spring in Mill Street. Arthur died at the age of forty-two leaving Susan with the Black Horse and five children. Susan later married Ben Billingham from Black Horse Lane, and later still the licence passed to Susan's daughter, Edith Allen, who kept it until the mid-1960s. *(Ossie Biddle Collection)*

Delph folk and regulars at the Black Horse in the 1950s. Left to right: Alf Allen (Mrs Hobson's son-in-law), Geoff Walker, Bert Fletcher (proprietor of Little Duchess Coaches of Wordsley), Hilda Walker, Lizzie Webb, Edith Allen (née Hobson) and Mary Fletcher (née Hobson, and wife of Bert). Mary was one of the five children of Susan Hobson – she was sister of Edith who eventually took over the licence of the Black Horse. *(Hilda Walker Collection)*

Obviously after a drink or two it was difficult to maintain a balanced approach to photographing the regulars of the Black Horse outside the pub, but the picture does provide a glimpse of the building with its original doorway between two bays – tap room to the left, bar to the right. Note the Truman, Hanbury & Buxton Brewery signs. *(Ossie Biddle Collection)*

The home of Ted and
Minnie Cartwright at
12 Black Horse Lane.
The Cartwrights ran their
newspaper-selling business
from here until about 1963.
Black Horse Lane was a
little world of its own – 'All
human life was there,' as
one local described it! People
remember the Dews, coal
merchants, the Cartwrights
and many others.
(Frank Bennett)

Ted Cartwright sitting outside his
house in Black Horse Lane – he
used to fetch the stock of papers
on his motorbike and Minnie
rode in the sidecar clutching an
umbrella on wet days to keep the
papers dry. *(Frank Bennett)*

Black Horse Lane, like The Goss, was cleared of its old houses in the 1960s, and as can be seen in this contemporary view, they have been replaced with modern houses, laid out in a more orderly manner. At one time the Cartwrights created their own right of way from their property to Corbett Road, but generally these roads have always been cul-de-sacs, or 'pudding bag' streets as we would say in the Black Country. *(John James)*

Dave Preston at his home in Delph Road in 2002. The building in the background was a mill – another survivor of the old Delph – sometimes also known as Nock's Mill (the Nock family once lived at Delph House). Dave still calls his property Delph Mill to this day. *(Ned Williams)*

A terrace of five and then three Victorian houses occupies the stretch of Delph Road between Delph Mill and Corbett Road. The latter is flanked by a matching pair of council 'semis' – just glimpsed on the left of the picture and probably dating from the mid-1930s, and part of the Corbett Road scheme. At one time these houses looked out across The Delph towards the mission church and Turk Street. *(Ned Williams)*

The Dock & Iron, seen here in 2007, has only been known by that name since 1985; it was previously the Duke William. The original Duke William stood on this site next door to the Delph Brewery – established by George Elwell in 1876. The brewery had to be abandoned about the time of the First World War as subsidence was causing its collapse. *(Ned Williams)*

The Goss today is still a quiet cul-de-sac off Delph Road, but is now flanked with 1970s housing. In earlier times only a row of small houses was to be found on the right-hand side. The road, once only a track, led to the lock-keeper's house adjacent to the original course of the Delph Locks. Two other isolated houses fronted the original course of the canal, now reached via a track from Corbett Road. (They are just visible in the picture on page 97). *(John James)*

The rarest of views! Looking from The Goss towards the back of Gaslight Terrace in Delph Road and the pit banks and 'frame' beyond, on the far side of the bottom of Turk Street in the 1950s. In the centre of the picture is Tinkers Cottage and part of a yard which was the remains of Bidmead's slaughterhouse. The Bidmeads ran a butcher's shop by Delph Bridge. *(Hilda Walker Collection)*

Jack Walker stands outside 124 Delph Road, his sister's home, in the 1950s. We are looking towards the junction with The Goss. Note how the terrace in the background has subsided and is now way below the level of the road. This was Gaslight Terrace. Two houses and two bungalows now stand on this site. Hilda and Jeff Walker moved into 124 Delph Road after getting married on 10 October 1953. At the time Silcox's shop was at the far end of the terrace, at no. 136, and Mrs Silcox owned most of the houses in the terrace. Horace and Dolly Harris lived at no. 134 – next door to the shop. No. 132 was occupied by Ian and Annie Lewis. Ian Lewis was a postman and caretaker at the Delph Mission Church. Jack and Polly Ward lived at no. 130, the last of the 'sunken' houses. Mrs Allen was at no. 128. No. 126 was occupied by various people (Mrs Smith, Mrs Dillard and the Barnbrooks). Hilda's brother, Albert Silcox, lived next door to at no. 122, but when he moved out, Derek and Margaret Homer moved in (see page 94). Originally these houses had been numbered from 9 to 23 in reverse order.

This view from 124 Delph Road was taken to record Hilda and the car but with hindsight we can see that it reveals the pit bank at the bottom of Turk Street and a frame above one of the fireclay pits (E.J. &J. Pearson's Pit no. 7).
(Hilda Walker)

In this later view of the remains of Fireclay Pit no. 7, Turk Street can actually be seen in the foreground – including some rather modern street lighting! Once, a short tramway ran from this pit straight into E.J. & J. Pearson's brickworks, crossing both Delph Lane and Turners Lane as it did so. *(Hilda Walker Collection)*

The general store at 122 (later no. 136) Delph Road was opened by Albert and Maria Elizabeth Higgs and sold everything from lamp oil to tobacco. Albert Higgs went on to become a Brierley Hill councillor. Albert and Maria's daughter, Elizabeth (later married to Charlie Silcox of Quarry Bank), was a nurse working nights at Wordsley Hospital during the Second World War, but that did not stop her from running the shop during the day. She continued to run it until the early 1960s. *(Hilda Walker Collection)*

Delph folk – regulars at the Stores – on a Sunday outing to the hop-yards. Left to right: Harry Marsden, Charlie Silcox, ? Roberts, Hilda Walker (née Silcox), Emmy Whittaker, Edith Smith, Roland Whittaker, and Tony Whittaker, plus, crouching in front, Joe Smith, a bookie's runner. *(Geoff Walker)*

MEMORIES OF THE DELPH: MARGARET HOMER, NÉE HARRIS

I was born at 11 (134) Delph Road in 1940, and my first nights would have been spent in the air raid shelter with my mother, Dolly Harris. Though she was afraid of the bombing, she was even more afraid of thunder and lightning and the following rain which often caused the house to flood. The carpets had to be got up and the furniture raised, the sideboard was permanently raised on moulded glass blocks. The house was part of Gaslight Terrace – a name which stuck even after electricity arrived in 1956. One of the first people to knock on the door after that was a vacuum-sweeper salesman and we bought our first electrical gadget.

My Dad, Horace, worked at Round Oak Steel Works at the blast furnace by day and as an air raid warden at night. My mother had worked at Stephens and Williams' glassworks, and then at Marsh & Baxter in the sausage room.

On Saturdays we collected flowers from the garden and took them round to the church. The church was well-attended by local people and I remember beetle drives in the winter and anniversary parades on Whit Sunday.

Noah and Emma Webb were based at the Stores, at the foot of the Delph Locks. Noah Webb ran a fleet of canal boats and Emma ran the pub. Emma is seen on the right of this picture some time in the early 1900s. On the left is a servant, holding Elizabeth – Emma's youngest daughter. The pub acted as a store for boatmen, hence the name. Noah outlived Emma, but died in 1924. It is thought the pub continued in this form for a few more years and was then demolished to make way for its replacement. *(Emma Hanglin Collection)*

The new version of the Stores looks a little sorry for itself in this 1950s view, taken from the wharf at the far side of the basin at the foot of the Delph Locks. The new building is thought to date from 1936. The original name lasted until 1986 when it became known as the Tenth Lock – despite the fact there are only eight locks in the present flight. *(Carol Cobb)*

The Tenth Lock as it is today, occupying its strategic site at the foot of the Nine Locks, of which there are eight! Today this is the centre of The Delph as the pub faces the junction with Turners Lane – once a minor byway into the scattered houses, pits and brickworks of The Delph, now access to the huge Withymoor Village. *(John James)*

Pat rests on a lock gate at the foot of the Delph Locks in 1970. From this angle it is apparent that the bottom lock is almost under Delph Road. The Stores is out of sight to the left and the small shop at the end of the wharf on the right has vanished but the view straight ahead was still dominated by E.J. & J. Pearson's Delph Brickworks at that date. *(Ned Williams)*

A view looking down the Delph Locks from Nine Locks Bridge, Mill Street, as a canal horse crosses the 'arm' which led to the original flight of locks, 1950s. The replacement had eight rather than nine! In the hazy distance we can glimpse the chimneys at Pearson's brickworks, and to the left are the canal houses close to Corbett Road, which once stood alongside the flight of locks. *(Bill Bawden)*

Holly and Prince turn a narrowboat at the foot of the Delph Locks on 7 June 2008 – part of celebrations to commemorate the 150th anniversary of the rebuilding of the Delph Locks. Note Delph Bridge beyond and the new houses now flanking Delph Road at this location. *(John James)*

E.J. & J. Pearson

Exploring The Delph in the twenty-first century makes great demands upon the imagination, for so little now remains to illustrate the complicated story of the area. Mines, works, the mission church, the gasworks, housing and little shops have all disappeared. Thankfully the canal and one or two roads still exist so that we can get our bearings and try to picture things as they once were, glimpsed in old photographs and maps, and recorded in assorted scraps of information.

Of all that has vanished, perhaps the Delph Works of E.J. & J. Pearson are the most significant – they were once a prominent feature of the local landscape and skyline. They were a major local employer and were involved in mining and brickmaking – the two human activities that shaped The Delph. Interestingly, they are also an enterprise that we know something about. When celebrating their centenary in 1960, the company made an effort to put its history on the record. Mr Elliott Evers, the company chairman, with the help of Col. Thomas, assembled the company's history and presented it in a long speech at the centenary dinner held at Dudley's Station Hotel on Saturday 7 May 1960.

Two brothers, John and William Pearson, established the business of E.J. & J. Pearson in 1860. They had it in mind to build up the company and pass it on to their sons, Edward Jukes Pearson, the son of John, and John Pearson Jnr, the son of William, hence the name of the firm. This is very much a tale involving family history so these names have to be set out clearly! In 1860 the Pearson brothers operated in partnership

The Delph Firebrick Works looking from Turners Lane towards Brierley Hill at the beginning of the twentieth century.

with other local businessmen, including a John Price – the head of a canal carrying firm based in Brierley Hill, and one-time manager of the Level Iron Works. However, we must not rush to the conclusion about the name Price which plays a later part in the story.

The business was mainly concerned with mining coal and fireclay, but the acquisition of the Delph Works launched them firmly into the brickmaking world. It was a brick works that had been previously worked by Messrs Harper & Moore, on a lease from the Earl of Dudley (the story does indeed become complicated because Messrs Moore and Harper were later absorbed by Pearsons). As well as the Delph Works, the company also worked the Tintam Abbey Works at The Thorns, Quarry Bank. In the 1870s the firm set up the Crown Works based on mines closer to Amblecote.

Another development of the 1870s was the appointment of J.W. Thomas as a partner in the firm. He was William Pearson's son-in-law. Although he came from Halifax, it is family connection that explains his appearance in the story. In 1883, Mr Thomas's son, Charles William Thomas, came on board. By the end of the 1880s the firm of E.J. & J. Pearson were entirely in the hands of the Thomas Family (father and son), now well-established members of Wesleyan Methodist circles in Stourbridge, and keen members of what eventually became the Territorial Army.

Charles Thomas brought a Territorial colleague into the firm by the name of Guy V. Evers. The Evers family was another important local entrepreneurial family based in Stourbridge. It was Charles Thomas and Guy Evers who greatly expanded the company and set it on its twentieth-century course. This process began with the expansion and rebuilding of the Delph Works. The nineteenth-century works was very much like the picture used on the centenary ashtrays (see page 102), bordered by the canal and Turner Road, with the large chimney dominating the landscape. The twentieth-century works was larger and is glimpsed in later photographs. Offices and laboratories, and an increased variety of workshops now contributed to the site. Guy Evers died in 1959 – a year short of the firm's centenary, but C.W. (Col.) Thomas was still alive at the age of ninety-three. He was not able to attend the centenary dinner but he was able to help Elliot Evers (Guy's son) compile the company's history.

Progress in the twentieth century was not straightforward. A serious fire in the Delph Mill during 1912 was a setback, but was used as an opportunity to modernise the works and to introduce electricity. The First World War stimulated growth and in 1916 the company took over the Canal Works, previously owned by a Mr Hickman. After that war, the company took over Messrs Harris & Pearson and then Harper & Moore's. By the 1930s E.J. & J. Pearson was the biggest firebrick manufacturer in the area.

Through two world wars and countless booms and recessions, E.J. & J. Pearson managed to remain profitable, produced a good product and employed many local people. In 1957 the firm amalgamated with J.T. Price & Co. of the Brettell Lane Brickworks and began a new era of trading as Price-Pearson Refractories Ltd. J.T. Price company was established in 1913 and owned several local brickworks including the Cricket Fields Works at Brettell Lane, the Leys Works at Brierley Hill, and the Planet Works at Kingswinford. Like other such enterprises it was very much a family firm. J.T. Price himself became MD of Price-Pearson Refractories until his retirement in about 1965 when Mr Elliot Evers took his place.

As the 1960s progressed, the new company set out to build a new works – the Albion Works – and thus began the decline of the Delph Works which, up until then, had been the hub of this mining and brickmaking empire. The company's offices moved to Moor Street.

In about 1966 the company withdrew from any further mining activity and concentrated on refractory brick manufacture. (There was some diversification – for example the old works at The Hayes had been replaced with a factory producing commercial vehicle trailers: M. & G. Trailers Ltd). The decade witnessed a decline in several local industries; particularly the metal industries and the demand for firebricks began to decline.

Derek Trickett, of Cradley, worked as an electrician for a contractor working at the Delph Works from 1956 until 1963, and from then until 1988 was employed by E.J. & J. Pearson themselves. He can provide an account of the final chapter in the life of the works. It seems that Price Pearson, as it had become, was taken over by J. & J. Dyson of Sheffield in 1972 and the works then operated as Dyson Refractories. The remains of the works were later used by a machine tool division of the Sheffield-based company.

When the Delph Works site closed in the 1980s it was not included in the area that was being open-cast mined for remaining deposits of coal (the large area behind the works on either side of the railway). The area once occupied by the works was flattened to make way for housing development – the Withymoor Village scheme.

The Delph was always regarded as a rough area plagued with poverty, and in which poor quality housing was forever threatened with subsidence. No doubt the locals saw it all differently! The pubs of The Delph were plentiful because they had to cope with the thirst of miners, brickyard workers and gas-workers, not forgetting the large number of boatmen who often rested at The Delph at weekends. Women singing and men fighting were a feature of life in The Delph on Saturday nights. On Sundays the wooden mission church came into its own!

Opposite, top: Price-Pearson directors at the Canal Works, Brettell Lane, in August 1961. Left to right: W.J. Price, J.R. Steel and R.E.G. Evers. *(W. Boyd Collection)*

Opposite, bottom: The Managing Director of Price-Pearson, Mr R.E.G. Evers, presents a fifty years' service medal to Mrs Rachael Diplock of Corbett Road, 15 May 1963. Such presentations regularly took place – see page 20 of *What's Happened to Quarry Bank?* – despite the popular view that brickyard work was unhealthy. Rachael came from a whole family of brickyard workers. *(W. Boyd Collection)*

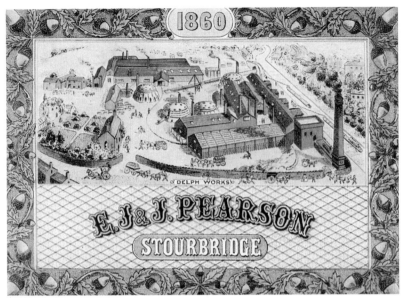

To celebrate the firm's centenary, this attractive print of the works was incorporated into the design of a commemorative glass ashtray (working with clay was supposed to have coated the linings of throat and lungs and made smoking safe!). Note that the picture illustrates the alignment of the firm's canal basin seen below. *(W. Boyd Collection)*

This evocative view of E.J. & J. Pearson's basin at the Delph Firebrick Works in the 1900s also provides a glimpse of the gasworks and public house and cottages on the far side of the canal. No trace of this basin can be found today. *(W.Boyd Collection)*

The E.J. & J. Pearson football team, possibly photographed just before the Second World War. Back row, left to right: J. Smith, J. Cotton, F. Biddlestone, A. Harper, T. Ince, G. Hickman, W. Winwood (Trainer). Middle row: F. Batham, (Secretary), J. Wood, H. Beaman, H. Leddington, S. Lunn, A. Cartwright (Manager). Front row: S. Longmore, F. Powell, and T. Wassell. *(W. Boyd Collection)*

A collection of attractively covered E.J. & J. Pearson catalogues preserved in Brierley Hill Library Collection.

An aerial view of The Delph in the late 1970s, showing the extent of the open-cast mining that drastically swept away the history of the area, and ultimately prepared it for the building of the Withymoor Village. The junction of Turners Lane and Delph Road can be seen on the left, just by Delph Bridge, and the canal and Lower Delph Road progresses diagonally across the picture. The latter meets the road descending from Brierley Hill at Silver End.

The demolition of the last chimney stack at E.J. & J. Pearson's Delph Brickworks. Between the chimney and the Chapel Street flats it is possible to make out the houses in Delph Road. (Carol Cobb)

Just beyond The Delph Bridge – sometimes remembered as the 'Yellow Bridge' – one comes to Rock's Hill, a steep short cut from The Delph up into Brierley Hill. Seen here in the 1950s the twenty-nine steps of Rock's Hill are surrounded by housing – all of which has long disappeared leaving the steps now very open. Rock's Hill led to Little Potter Street at the junction with Hill Street. In the latter was a small Methodist chapel used by some of the inhabitants of The Delph who found the local mission too obviously Anglican. The Baptists were not far away in South Street and had a spectacular hillside graveyard stretching down to Delph Road.

Looking down Rock's Hill in the late 1970s we see that the surrounding housing has vanished. At the foot of the steps is the Bell public house and to the right is the end gable of The Delph Post Office. Dominating the picture is Pearson's Delph Firebrick Works, beyond which is the open-cast mining, and on the skyline is the Amblecote Road close to the Birch Tree pub. *(Dave Galley)*

Above: The terrace of houses to the left of Rock's Hill (going up), photographed in September 1961. At the time the Chapel Street redevelopment scheme was still being planned but these houses were not going to stand here much longer. Note the lamp post in Rock's Hill. *(Express & Star)*

Looking from the right-hand side of Rock's Hill straight across Rock's Hill itself towards the back of the terrace seen above. This 1950s picture features Ann Timmins, who lived on Rock's Hill, and her sister Lily. The way in which these terraces were built at right angles to the steep slope of Rock's Hill is very clear.

Above: By September 1963 the houses on the right-hand side of Rock's Hill had been abandoned and were awaiting demolition. *(Express & Star)*

Pat Cochran and her pet dog sit outside one of the houses on the right-hand side of Rock's Hill in the 1950s. *(Carol Cobb)*

The Rock Tavern at the top of Rock's Hill is now closed but the front portion is used as a fish and chip shop serving the Chapel Street estate. *(Ned Williams)*

Before we return to our trek along Delph Road, let's have one last look at the way in which the Chapel Street area of Brierley Hill towers over the area occupied by The Delph. Here we see the children of Mill Street Junior School dressed to take part in *The Pied Piper of Hamelin*, in 1952, standing in the school playground. Above them we see The Promenade. The houses on the right still stand. Children from The Delph did attend this school – for example Ann Timmins (Jnr) on the right lived in the fish and chip shop next to the Bell. *(Carol Cobb)*

Today there is a small layby between the Delph Bridge and the Bell by the canal pound at the foot of the locks, but there was once a small 'island' at this location. At one time there was a police box on the island but here it has been replaced by a bench where Ann Timmins from Rock's Hill, on the right, is sitting with her daughter Joyce and sister Winnie. The picture was taken in the early 1950s and shows the building which may once have been an office for the canal wharf, but is better remembered as a butcher's shop. *(Joyce Bissell)*

The Bell, Delph Road, 2008. Note the entrance to Rock's Hill on the right. *(John James)*

Four 1930s houses in Lower Delph Road, 2007. The one on the right was The Delph Post Office – commemorated by the continuing existence of the postbox in the pillar in front of the house. At one time the post office had been on the other side of the road but moved into this building in the late 1930s and was first looked after by Mr Swain, who later moved to the office in Quarry Bank High Street. Subsequent names associated with this office include Hobson and Maybury. Between the post office and the Bell was a fish and chip shop run by Mr and Mrs Tom Timmins. From 1947 until closure in 1957 it was run by their son Tom and his wife Gwen. *(John James)*

DELPH GASWORKS

The Brierley Hill District Gaslight Company was authorised in 1865 and supplied gas from the Delph Gasworks to a wide area until 1931 when it merged with the Dudley Gaslight Company. The site at The Delph must have been ideal, as it was adjacent to the canal. Following nationalisation in 1949, gas production was concentrated at larger works and small works became simply holders of gas. Once the gasworks became redundant it was demolished by Tony Whittaker and the site became home to an industrial estate.

Between the gasworks' wharf and the Delph Bridge was a row of houses inhabited by gasworkers, and at the bottom of Gas Street was a pub called The Duncan. John Corbett, the 'Salt King', is thought to have had a canal wharf and business in this area but this was sold in 1853 when John left to make his fortune from salt at Droitwich.

Looking back towards Brierley Hill across The Delph in the 1950s – before the Chapel Street flats were built and changed the landscape forever. Note how St Michael's Church and Marsh & Baxter's factories dominate the skyline at this time. The Firebrick Works are lost in the hollow but the gas holders at the gasworks are clearly visible. The houses on Lower Delph Road stretch to the left. *(Express & Star)*

In this mid-1980s aerial view of The Delph, the Chapel Street flats now dominate the landscape, but the picture clearly illustrates the course of Delph Road, from the canal bridge on the right, curving round the site of the gasworks and heading left for Silver End. New houses around Heronswood Road occupy the site of Pearsons' brickworks, bottom right. The Delph Locks can be seen clearly on the right, and the course of Rock's Hill shows up well. *(Stan Hill Collection)*

Although pictures of the gasworks at The Delph have proved impossible to find, several family pictures from that area add to our knowledge of that part of The Delph. Here are Elizabeth Jones and her five daughters on the steps of Stratford House in 1906. Stratford House was the gasworks manager's home, and Elizabeth's husband, William Charles Jones, was manager from about 1903 until his retirement in 1933. He was born in Yorkshire in 1866 and joined the gas company at their Kingswinford Works before coming to The Delph. Apparently Elizabeth liked village life in The Delph despite the reputation of the area. Will Jones was a keen photographer, although relatively few of his pictures survive in good condition. *(Doreen Rutter)*

James and Ellen Aston and their six daughters lived in Delph Villa, which was right next door to the gasworks in Lower Delph Road. James, born in 1858, looked after Bantock's horses operating from a canal wharf at Brettell Lane, until he was killed in a road accident during the First World War. All six daughters married railwaymen – Nell, front left, married a railway guard called Fred Gallier, cornetist and sometime conductor of the Quarry Bank Silver Band. *(Margaret Exley)*

Returning to the centre of The Delph (the canal bridge) we now have to explore the area that filled a triangle between Turk Street, Turner's Lane and Amblecote Road. Turk Street left Delph Road opposite the Stores (the Tenth Lock) and eventually led to the Amblecote Road, close to a pub called the Grand Turk. A few yards up Turk Street was the Delph Mission Church, at a crossroads where a footpath crossed Turk Street. The alignments of these rights of way can still be traced today although the church has long since vanished. It is seen here in its original condition. Subsequently a church hall was built across the back of the building. Turk Street would be on the right. *(MPLHG Collection)*

THE CHURCH OF THE GOOD SHEPHERD

The little wooden Mission Church was dedicated to the Good Shepherd in 1886 and brought the Anglican Church into The Delph. No Nonconformist chapel had been provided but there were Methodist chapels of various kinds close by, and the Baptists were represented at South Street, Brierley Hill. Mission churches often work in a very chapel-like style and the Good Shepherd was no exception. It soon had a thriving Sunday School and was the centre of a host of weekday activities. By the late 1890s the curate-in-charge (the Revd George Tomlinson) felt that such intensive use of the building had reached the stage where a proper and separate Sunday School building was required.

By 1904, when the Revd Mr Pleming was in charge, it seemed a better idea to build a new church and use the temporary wooden building as the Sunday School and Institute. A building fund was started and struggled on for nearly half a century!

When the Church of England wanted to build a new church in the Hawbush area, the Rector of Brierley Hill hoped he would be able to use the Delph Church's Building Fund. This started a long-standing battle in which the Delph trustees tried to hang onto their own funds and hold on to the dream of building their own new church.

During the time when the end of the Second World War was approaching, the three ageing trustees of the Delph Church took stock of the situation. The funds now held over £5,000 and another £1,000 was represented in artefacts owned by the mission. However, the Rector of Brierley Hill was not inclined to appoint a replacement minister at The Delph and it seemed that the mission was deemed to have no future. After meetings between the trustees and the rector, advice was taken from an ecclesiastical lawyer and the Delph's fund was transferred to the guardianship of the Lichfield Diocesian Trust. The transfer took place in 1945 and it was believed that the funds could still only be used for the purpose for which they were collected.

By now the little wooden mission was showing signs of age. It was surrounded by buildings badly affected by subsidence caused by mining, but it seemed more likely that the wind might someday blow the church down. Steel ropes were strung over the church and made fast to the ground, thus tying the church down.

Although still fairly busy, the mission was doomed, and it closed in 1952. All the fund-raising and dreams of replacing it seemed to have come to nothing.

GUARDIANS OF THE GOOD SHEPHERD

The church in The Delph survived partly as a result of enthusiastic supporters – two of which were dogged in their commitment to the place even though neither of them lived in The Delph!

Monthly church magazines from the Delph Mission, 1900s.

Joseph Dunn lived at South Lea on the Amblecote Road and was organist and choirmaster in The Delph for many years. He was born in 1861 and joined the Great Western Railway on the clerical side at Brettell Lane station in 1877. He was promoted to Chief Clerk at Withymoor (Netherton Goods) in 1891 where he was eventually tempted to leave the railway and take up work at Hingleys Ironworks. He retired from there in 1945 at the age of eighty-five! He learnt the art of playing the organ at Christ Church, Quarry Bank, where he followed C.H. Hawkeswood as organist. However, he transferred his allegiance to The Delph in about 1893.

As well as playing the organ and conducting the choir, he was at various times secretary, treasurer and trustee of the little church. When he died in February 1951, the Rector of Brierley Hill (the Revd Mr Crowther Green) conducted his funeral at The Delph although the burial had to take place at St Michaels.

The other champion of the Good Shepherd was Francis Lane of Crescent Avenue, Brierley Hill. He was born in 1875 and grew up to become a mining engineer. He founded his own company at the Lanwill Works in Brierley Hill, having gained experience as a plant manager for E.J. & J. Pearson at the Crown Works and Homer Hill. He had mining interests at Grendon Colliery at Atherstone, in South Wales and elsewhere. He also had artistic skills and an interest in music and was President of Brierley Hill Choral Society.

Beside all these activities, Francis Lane developed a devotion to the little church in The Delph. When it was dedicated back in 1886 he was singing in the choir. He became a Sunday School teacher, then Superintendent, then a lay preacher. By the time he had become a trustee of the Good Shepherd he was an enthusiastic fund-raiser, amassing money to rebuild the church. He fought hard to try to make sure the funds could be used for no other purpose, but when he died in January 1946 it must have seemed that the church was never going to be replaced. His memorial service was held at The Delph, but like Joseph Dunn, he had to be buried at St Michael's, Brierley Hill.

A plaque in memory of Francis Lane is to be found in St Michael's Church and this does record his devotion to the Good Shepherd Mission Church.

From a painted portrait of Francis Lane.
(June Bowen)

Sunday School teachers and scholars at the Good Shepherd Mission Church in The Delph in about 1910. Back row, left to right: Miss Rowley, -?-, Miss A. Shaw (later Mrs Sidaway), Miss E. Stevens, Miss Parrish, Miss Pargeter, and Miss Rogers. Seated on front row: Miss Benson, Miss E. Shaw (later Mrs Sidaway), Miss M. Benson, Miss A. Bill, Miss S. Stevens, and Miss P. Hartland. The two Miss Shaws are sisters but although they both became Mrs Sidaway, their husbands were not related. *(From the collection of the late Mrs Doris Peat)*

More Memories of The Delph

Ann Timmins and Cynthia Garrett became childhood friends in The Delph, and are still friends today. Ann was born at 8 Lower Delph Road where her parents, Tom and Gwen, were proprietors of the fish and chip shop next to the Bell. Cynthia lived at 44 Lower Delph Road and her father, Arthur, was well known as the lamp lighter. He worked all his life for the Gas Company and checked the lights from The Delph to Netherton. After the war he was given a pick-up van complete with ladder, and the girls loved to ride around with him – especially at a time when very few people had cars!

Several people still alive today remember the canal bridge being widened and rebuilt in the early 1930s, but the exact date has not been identified. Similarly, several people recall a small chapel by the bridge – used as a Sunday School. It may have been demolished when the bridge was rebuilt – no precise information has been found. Others remember the cottages inhabited by the gasworkers. Some had bells fitted that could be rung when a fitter was wanted in the works. Pubs, houses, a chapel and the gasworks themselves, have all disappeared.

Growing Up in Turk Street: Lynda Laker (née Poole)

For a five-year period as a young child I lived in the very heart of The Delph. My family (Mom, Dad, and younger sister) lived at 8 Turk Street in what had once been a Midland Red single-decker bus. A condition of purchasing and residing in the bus was that we had to change the colour, remove the engine, and take off the wheels. Home had to be a horrible sludgy green!

As a five-year-old I accepted this as quite normal, and it wasn't until I was much older that I realised my popularity at school was something to do with being able to invite my friends to tea in the bus – and the fact that Mom made a mean strawberry trifle.

My home was situated in a field, perched on the brow of a small bank, on land adjacent to Mrs Cartwright's house – all belonging to the Earl of Dudley. From our viewpoint we looked down onto the track leading from the claypit from whence the lorries, heavily laden, lumbered up and down in the direction of Turners Lane. While we were there the remaining pits were wound down. The pit bonks became my playground.

Turk Street was a lane, just dirt and gravel, surrounded by hedgerows choked with convolvulus and sweet-smelling dog roses. Harold Thompson, the local tramp who slept at the brickworks, was a daily sight, and I remember the old church which was dark, brooding and empty until it was demolished. Some fifty years on, the Withymoor Village housing estate covers my old stamping ground and I look back to life in the bus with nostalgia.

Fred, Kathryn, Lynda and Phoebe enjoying life around their bus-based home at 8 Turk Street in 1952. *(Lynda Laker)*

Fred, with Rolly, the family's dog, emerges from the shed-like extension made to the family's home – an ex-Midland Red bus. It seems to have been a SOS or ON/DON type vehicle introduced by Midland Red in 1934 and much-admired at the time for its curvaceous bodywork and radiused corners to the windows. As can be seen here, the emergency exit was in the centre of the rear of the bus.

Lynda and Kathryn Poole play in the garden of their home at 8 Turk Street. The house in the background was occupied by Mrs Cartwright. Lynda's father laid out a smart garden around his bus. *(Lynda Poole)*

Below: The crossroads in Turk Street survives today in footpath form. The church was just to the right. *(John James)*

The line of Gayfield Avenue being laid out in 1975 as preparations for building the Withymoor Village begin. The fence crossing the centre of the picture marks the line of Turk Street. In the distance is Pearson's brickworks. *(Derek Homer)*

GROWING UP IN TURK STREET: DEREK HOMER

I had a wonderful childhood growing up in Turk Street, it was like being in the country but within easy reach of the town. There were two houses near the top, six in the middle and three at the very bottom, though why it was called a street is beyond me, it was actually a dirt track – wide enough for a vehicle at the top, then narrowing to a path and then widening out again towards the bottom, where one came to the church.

One of my first memories was of going two hundred yards down the lane to watch pit ponies being brought up from underground at the end of their shift. It was fascinating for a child of four or five and I could have watched all day. There was a small field behind the pit that had a pool where frogspawn and newts could be found. In the winter, after a fall of snow, we would all gather in the field with a steep slope with toboggans our fathers had made – and we wouldn't go home until it was dark. In the summer we built dens in the hedges.

My grandparents lived in a farmhouse just a little way down Turk Street and it had been a working farm when my father was a boy; his job had been to deliver the milk. Like every other building in The Delph, the farmhouse, which had been in the family a long time, was affected by subsidence and was eventually demolished.

Turk Street, Delph Lane and Turners Lane joined Delph Road separately and in quick succession just before the canal bridge. Each took the adventurous visitor deep into The Delph landscape of scattered houses, smallholdings, pits, pit banks and fields. Between Turk Street and Delph Lane was the site of Pit no. 7, the frame and pit-bank surviving until the 1970s. Between Delph Lane and Turners Lane were the remains of an air raid warden's shelter, which became a home to Harold Thompson, the famous local tramp. On the right of Turners Lane was The Delph Brickworks, but on the left were fields from which this picture was taken in the early 1970s. Turners Lane is just out of the picture to the right and we look towards the houses once inhabited by the Hills, then the Taylors, and behind them the Edwards. The houses were demolished to make way for the new Withymoor Village but some of the trees remain. *(Dave Galley)*

MARION'S STORY

Marion Prosser was born at 38 Lockside, The Goss, in 1928, the youngest of twelve. She remembers space being at a premium in the three-bedroom house, four to a bed being the norm! Despite the lack of space, everyone sat down to eat – though not all at the same time. They were happy days and they all looked out for each other. Marion attended Mount Pleasant School (see photo on page 69) and at dinnertime had to take her older brother's meals to John Hall's brickyard in Turners Lane. Every child had a special job and Marion's was preparing huge piles of bread for Sunday tea, and polishing the brasses every Thursday.

Marion's father drowned in the canal one foggy morning in 1943, and ten years later Marion's nephew met the same fate. Her mother, Sarah, once saved a child from drowning in the canal by extending a wooden washing line prop to him. This was the reality of living by the canal.

The watch given to Dolly after thirty-nine years' work in local bakeries.

Dolly Beech at 223 Delph Road on 9 August 2007 – her 100th birthday.

MEMORIES OF THE DELPH: DOLLY BEECH

Dolly was born on 9 August 1907 at 29 Mount Pleasant, Quarry Bank. She was a niece of both Jack and George Dunn, both of whom, at separate times, ran bakeries in Mount Pleasant. Dolly went to Mount Pleasant School – just across the road – and then went to work in Uncle Jack's bakery. In 1935 Dolly married policeman Charles Beech and then went to live in a new house in Delph Road.

Charles Beech died six years later and Dolly decided to go back to work at her uncle's bakery, and she stayed in this job until her retirement. In the meantime, Dunn's Bakery had been absorbed by Darby's Bakery of Brettell Lane (like Robert's, of the Delph Bakery) and Darbys was then absorbed by the Rank Hovis McDougall group.

For many years Dolly was the only female driver for the bakery, and in fact, continued to drive her own car until she was eighty-nine.

MEMORIES OF THE DELPH: RENIE LEDDINGTON

Renie was born on 4 October 1918 at 8 Black Horse Lane, the third daughter of James and Blanche Leddington. James worked at Stevens & Williams as a glassmaker, and their home was a two-up, two-down house with a shared yard and toilet.

Renie remembers fetching the groceries from Miss Lawton's shop in Delph Road: a penn'uth of this, and a happ'uth of that! She also fetched coal from Mr and Mrs Dews who sold it from a shed built on to their premises near the Bull & Bladder (next to Roberts's Bakery.) In 1926 there was an all-out strike and Renie's father was out of work so she joined the family picking slack and bits of coal from pit banks, keeping an eye open for the local bobby. They were always hungry and sometimes would go down to the fields in The Delph and eat the leaves of hawthorn bushes.

Like many others, Renie can remember the Cartwrights (Ted and Minnie) who lived at the top of Black Horse Lane. They sold newspapers by standing on either side of Mill Street. Eventually they had a shop above the Stores.

Renie went to Mount Pleasant School and reached it by 'going through the Bog-Hole' – a row of old-fashioned toilets behind the houses in Black Horse Lane, across 'the lezzer' (a field) and out into Mill Street, passing a sweet shop and a blacksmith's. Later, Renie went to the Intermediate School in Brierley Hill.

Renie recalls, 'My earliest memories are of going to the little wooden church in the middle of The Delph, the Good Shepherd. When I was a little older I used to go with my sisters three times every Sunday. I loved the anniversaries and the summer outing, usually to Clent or Kinver. Once we travelled by canal boat which was all trimmed up with red, white and blue bunting. And at Christmas there was a party, with a present for everyone. I remember Mr Francis Lane and Mr Dunn, the organist.'

Some members of the Mount Pleasant Local History Group pause by a tank while exploring The Delph in 2008. *(John James)*

6

QUARRY BANK FOLK

MIKE HOLDER (1944–2008)

Mike Holder was born in Sheffield Street and attended Quarry Bank Infants and
Primary Schools. From 1956 to 1959 he attended the Boys' Secondary School in
Coppice Lane. In 1960 he joined the Police and spent more than thirty years in the
service. In 1964 he was presented with the Duke of Edinburgh's Award Scheme Gold
Medal. He served as a Detective Superintendent at Sandwell from 1985 to 1987 and in
the 1990s was Divisional Commander in Dudley.

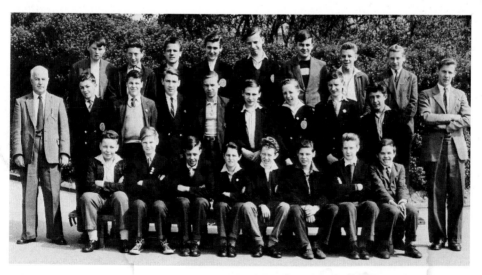

Mike Holder is the fifth pupil from the left in this 1959 form 3A picture taken at Coppice Boys'
Secondary School. On the left is the headmaster, Mr Jeavons, and on the right is his form
teacher, Philip Millward, who provided the text on Mike Holder, and this picture.

On retirement from the Police he became a highly respected figure in the security industry, forming the successful Cougar Monitoring Company in Cradley Heath. A tough spokesman on crime, he also advised hundreds of businesses on how to protect themselves against criminals in his role as Director of Dudley Borough Business Crime Partnership. He became a member of Home Office committees dealing with crime prevention. In addition he served as President of the Black Country Chamber of Commerce, was President of Brierley Hill Rotary Club, sat on the Board of Directors of Dudley Zoo, and was involved in the St Thomas' Network.

In later years Mike Holder served as a governor at his old school – which, by then, had become Thorns College. He became a firm friend of the college and in 1992 was immensely proud to be asked to officially open a new teaching block. A plaque in the reception office records this.

Many in the Black Country, and particularly in the business community and his former police colleagues, were left shocked by the news of Mike's sudden death in October 2008. At his funeral in Old Hill, over 600 people attended to pay their respects. A stroke unit dayroom in A2 ward at Russells Hall Hospital will be dedicated to Mike, and the Mike Holder Trust has been established to help disadvantaged young people – a cause close to his heart. Mike was a kind man, willing to help those in need. The trust was launched at 'A Night for Mike' function when £3,000 was raised by two hundred people who gathered to celebrate his life.

Mike Holder was very proud of his Black Country origins and, above all, his Quarry Bank roots.

Geoff Tristram

Geoffrey Tristram was born in 1954 in Victoria Road, Quarry Bank. Shortly after he was born, Geoff and his father and mother, Len and Ruby, moved to a new council house in Anne Road. A few years later the Birch Coppice pub was built opposite their house. Meanwhile, when Geoff was three-and-a half, he gained a brother, David. The boys were very close and spent their childhood riding their bikes, cleaning out the hamster cage, playing Subbuteo and staging plays dressed up in their parents' clothing. Most of the time they were laughing uncontrollably. At weekends they were often to be found at their grandparents' house in Thorns Avenue (grandma and granddad were Bertha and Reuben Billingham).

Geoff attended Quarry Bank Primary Infants' and Junior Schools. At school he was a prodigious and enthusiastic artist and musician. From an early age he had spent much of his time drawing hundreds of pictures with his thirteen-colour biro. Although not especially academic, he passed his 11-plus and went to Tipton Grammar School. After that he studied at Wolverhampton College of Art, and gained a degree in Illustration and Graphic Design.

During this period he undertook many freelance illustration commissions, and after a year he became a full-time freelance artist and cartoonist, eventually working for the likes of the BBC, Embassy World Snooker, Penguin Books, Trivial Pursuit, and the Crown Agents. He has drawn and painted celebrities such as Ian Botham, Alan Shearer, Ian Hislop and Gary Lineker, and almost every famous snooker player. Many book covers, stamps and album sleeves have been commissioned from him.

Geoff Tristram (centre, clutching his books), surrounded by members of the History Group during a visit in the autumn of 2008. *(John James)*

In addition, Geoff has now written nine comedy novels featuring a chaotic and accident-prone artist called David Day. His childhood memories, and the schooldays spent in Quarry Bank, have inspired such novels as *A Bump on the Head*, and the prequel, *The Hunt for Grandad's Head*.

Meanwhile, what happened to that younger brother? David went on to Dudley Grammar School and then to Birmingham University where he studied English and Music. He is now a well-known comedy playwright, and his work is staged all over the world. He also runs an audio-visual business.

Hubert Symonds (Quarry Bank Funeral Director from 1928–70)

Hubert, or 'Bert' as he was more popularly known, was born in February 1900. His family had moved to the area from Herefordshire in the 1840s and had been established as funeral directors in Quarry Bank since 1858. Bert took over his father's business in 1928, operating from the family home: a terraced house at 40 Queen Street. The house was demolished in the 1970s to make way for new sheltered housing.

In 1933 Bert married Evelyn Court and they set up home in a rented mid-terrace house in King Street, then known as no. 8, but now known as no. 27. Bert constructed a new workshop at the bottom of the garden. He was not the only funeral director in the area and there was never enough demand to provide him with such work full-time. Consequently he took on other carpentry work to supplement his income. He never owned his own funeral vehicles and therefore hired them from other operators such

Evelyn, John and Bert Symonds, photographed in 1987. *(Family collection)*

as J.T. Brookes (up to 1959) and Charles Taylor (from 1959 to 1970). He never drove and for the first twenty years of trading he did not even have a telephone.

Working from home, with his wife always on hand to take orders, Bert made his coffins from oak or elm using only hand tools. He polished them and affixed the metal coffin furniture – all quite skilled work. He made all the funeral arrangements and aimed to conduct the funerals in a dignified way. Up until 1948, most local funerals concluded with an interment of the body as the nearest crematoria were in Birmingham.

Although the number of deaths varied from one period to another, Bert averaged between fifteen and twenty funerals in a full year, which means that in the forty-two years he was in business he conducted around seven hundred funerals altogether. One of these, in July 1946, was the funeral of the Revd William McCarthy – the only former vicar of Quarry Bank to be interred in Quarry Bank churchyard.

Like most of his generation, Bert was very hard-working. Independent funeral directors like Bert are now few and far between – in a manner of speaking, they are a 'dying' breed!

Philip Millward

Philip was born in Victoria Road, within the sound of the church bell, and therefore a true Quarry Banker. He was a pupil of the Infants' School in the High Street and he then attended the County Primary School at the time when Andrew Cooper was the headmaster. Philip was a choirboy at Christ Church and later became a Sunday School teacher there. Subsequent to passing the 11-plus, he went to King Edward's Grammar School in Stourbridge. Having achieved good results there, he left in 1958.

Philip was a keen footballer and played for Dunns Bank Rovers (1957/58) and during that season also played for Wolves at Molineux and Fellows Park, Walsall. Incredible though it might seem today, aged only eighteen, and without any formal qualifications, he was given a teaching job at the Coppice Lane Boys' School. His class was 1B and his responsibility was to teach the whole syllabus to the forty-five lads in this form. By Christmas he was teaching English and Maths to the fourth-year leaving class of thirty-nine boys. He was not very much older than his students, most of whom were close neighbours!

In 1966, Philip went to St Peter's College in Saltley to study Maths, and then returned to Quarry Bank to continue teaching. The senior boys' and senior girls' schools had by then amalgamated and were in new premises – Thorns School. Philip went on to become Head of Maths, Lower School Head, and eventually Senior Tutor. Most importantly, every young person under his care respected him and responded to his firm, fair, caring approach. Moreover, he remembered the name of every student under his tuition.

Although he retired from the teaching staff in 1993, he kept his connections with Thorns College and helped the school forge links with local industry. Lately Philip has been involved with education in Quarry Bank in the form of the Home and Hospital Tuition Service. He did this for fourteen years, finally retiring in 2008. He was a school governor at Thorns College for eight years and retains a firm interest in the school. He is a Quarry Banker to be proud of!

Philip Millward at Thorns in 1987. *(MPLHG)*

ACKNOWLEDGEMENTS

The Mount Pleasant Local History Group has seen its membership change over the years. Therefore the present members wish to thank all past members – many of whom will have added to the knowledge used to assemble this book. This means we thank: Olive Allchurch, Ossie Biddle, Doreen Cartwright, Bessie Cranton, Gladys Davies, Bram and Vera Dunn, Roy Smith, Jane Geddes, Pat Mattocks, Janice Mills, Charmayne Redding, Patrick and Sylvia Shaw, Ira and Sandra Hampton, Raymond Lilley, Gary Marshall, Lorraine Parkes, Walter Perks, Fred Tipton, Colin Southall, plus the late members: Horace Dunn, John Robinson, Arthur Pearson, Doris Peat, Jessie Yorke, Joyce Parkes and Emma Hanglin.

A brief glance at the acknowledgements in our previous publications will demonstrate that we have consulted hundreds of people over the last ten years and we cannot list them all again. However, there are many people who have helped us in the last two or three years while we have been working with this book in mind. Thanks therefore to the following: Marion Prosser, Eric Timmins, Samuel Homer, Dolly Beech, Joan Price, Lynda Laker, Ann Timmins, Renie Fisher, Dennis and Margaret Perks, Mike and Pat Atkin, Emma Webb, Pat Robinson, Andrew Pearson, John Symonds, Geoff and David Tristram, Keith Hodgkins, Philip Millward, Stan Hill, Margaret Roussell, Alan South, Arthur Pearson, Margaret Gallier, Doreen Ruttter, Connie Phillips, Hilda Walker, Frank Bennett and Roger Crombleholme. Thanks also go to the folks at each of Quarry Bank's churches, the shops and the pubs, to library staff at Stourbridge, Brierley Hill and the Dudley Archives, the editor of the *Express & Star* and folks at the *Black Country Bugle*, plus the head and staff at Mount Pleasant School. We know that we have talked to so many people and sought help from so many organisations that our list is bound to be incomplete so please accept our apologies if we have failed to mention you by name.

NAMING NAMES!

Marion Prosser has been able to identify most of the children in the picture printed on page 69. As there was no room to supply all the names in the caption we have added them here, just in case you need to know! Back row, left to right: John Allchurch, Derek Brown, Jack Hughes, Ken ?, Geoff Maiden, Roy Hazlewood, Tom Jennings, Harry Bailey, Dennis Whiley, Stanley Wood, Brian Shepherd. Next row: Edna Mole, Elsie Bolton, Joyce Thompson, Nellie Mullett, Irene Taylor, Aida Bache, Marion Prosser, Pat Dudley, Kathy Collins, Pearl Perrins. Third row: Audrey?, Alice Whittaker, ? Higgs, Jean Gennard, ? McColl, Brenda Thompson, Betty Dickens, Dorothy Round, -?-, Beryl Whomack, Nancy ?, Betty Round, Mary Freeman, Doris Green, Mary Castree, Hazel Brindley. Front row: David Cranape, Harry Whiley, Ken Collins, Reg Walton, Harcourt Field and Jimmy Williams.